Falling Short

A comedy

James Robson

Samuel French — London
New York - Toronto - Hollywood

ISBN 0 573 01763 8

Please see page iv for further copyright information

FALLING SHORT

First produced at The Old Meeting House, Helmsley, Yorkshire on 22nd November 1995 with the following cast of characters:

Giles Short	Adrian Roberts
Verity Short	Gillian Roberts
Frances Feldman	Alison Schofield
Trish Evans	Rosalind de Aragues
Fergus Rutherford	Martin Vander Weyer
Font Cairns	Howard Burnham
Hava Jaffa	David Powley
Monty	Robin Andrews
Adrian Smethers	Charles Saggers
Melissa Smethers	Cal Stockbridge
Gillette	Steve Hick
Workers	Christine Price, Moira Wood

Directed by Glyn Price

CHARACTERS

Giles Short
Verity Short
Frances Feldman
Trish Evans
Fergus Rutherford
Font Cairns
Hava Jaffa
Monty
Adrian Smethers
Melissa Smethers
Gillette
3 Workers (non-speaking)

SYNOPSIS OF SCENES

The action takes place in Giles' office at Rutherford's in Covent Garden, London

ACT I
    SCENE 1. 6 a.m.
    SCENE 2. 9 a.m.
    SCENE 3. 11.30 a.m.
    SCENE 4. 3 p.m.

ACT II
    SCENE 1 About 3.30 p.m.
    SCENE 2 Two hours later

Time—early 1990s

CHARACTERS

Giles Short Aged 44. Successful fiction editor to a small and once distinguished London publishing house called Rutherford's. Essentially a very likeable, dry, witty, kind, rather conservative (but with a daring streak) thoughtful man. Happy to take the path of least resistance most of the time, he is stubborn and tenacious when set upon a course of action; a man of his word. A perfectionist and idealist with pride and ambition who would hate to hurt anyone in the normal run of things. An urbane, neat and honourable man who would seem to have everything life can offer — but retains an undertow of sadness, lack of fulfilment.

Verity Short His wife, aged 37. To all appearances the better half of an ideal glossy couple. A nice intelligent "gel" from the Shires who has made a niche for herself in literary society of the not too radical kind. Superb wife, hostess, companion, she expects a lot from life — and her husband — and is rather smug and snobbish. Brimming with certainties, content, and zest, she is almost jolly, and jolly demanding at times. Childless by choice.

Frances Feldman (Fran) aged 37. Giles' secret long-term lover. An intense, intellectual, romantic dark lady of the Sonnets. Publishers' reader and frustrated writer as neurotically demanding and heavy as Verity is cheerfully four-square and light. Jewish/American maybe, rather histrionic and slightly predatory.

Trish Evans Giles' secretary, aged 30. A working-class Londoner with a funny phoney accent (sort of Pinner under Sloaney). Beautiful in an understated breathy way, shapely, simple, kind and uncomplicated by nature. Has a sharp sense of humour, an aged gran, and is more than a little fond of Giles.

Fergus Rutherford Chairman of Rutherford's, publisher, pushing 60. A once tough, abrasive Scot now mellowing sadly, pickled in Scotch, but still peppery at times. A minor poet of the Hugh McDiarmid school now feeling compromised and embittered by changes in publishing and public taste. Fond of Giles in a fatherly way. Shortsighted.

Font Cairns The flawed jewel in Rutherford's' crown, aged about 60. Best-selling author of bloody thrillers; a shrewd, manipulative, nasty old queen. Aware of his power and importance, florid but not flamboyantly gay. Bitchy, mannered, insecure, dangerous.

Hava Jaffa Czech, aged 65. Immensely wealthy entrepreneur and royalty-worshipping crook with a sporting streak and a peculiar code of honour forged in the fires of hell. Sentimental about his adopted country, an

Anglophile more "English" and better mannered than most Englishmen. Embodies a sense of having come through horrors, a man of dark presence and weight and strength. He wears several gold rings on both hands and always carries an orange which he tosses and toys with.

Monty Cockney doorman/security guard at Rutherford's, elderly. A fat, famous little bore whose conversation makes people want to run away/ commit suicide/hide in a cupboard/resign their job, etc. Old soldier, ex-POW, he is a stickler for rules, details, trivia, and beneath his precise sycophantic exterior is fascistic and unpleasant. About to retire. He has the curious habit of ending sentences with "n'cetera".

Adrian Smethers Children's fiction editor at Rutherford's, aged mid 20s. Fancies himself as a "bit of a card" and ladies' man. Wears fancy pullovers, red braces, trendy specs and Armani suits or jeans, maybe even sports a pony tail. Full of bubbling bonhomie and not altogether genuine brio and sincerity. Is really rather insecure and desperately grateful to, and envious of, Giles. But he totally adores his wife.

Melissa Smethers His wife, aged 25. A lovely loose-limbed chatterbox. Sweet natured but slightly sly and tactless. Worked at Rutherford's for a while, on and off, as a temporary typist/secretary. Heavily pregnant.

Gillette Aged about 55. Walking accident trying to happen. A cat burglar no longer up to the heights. Oft-failed suicide and vagrant, filthy, alcoholic, seriously droll, funny but with a broken heart. Welsh?

3 Workers London suburban types who work at Rutherford's.

Other plays by James Robson
published by Samuel French Ltd

Beulah
Mail Order Bride

ACT I

SCENE 1

Giles' office at Rutherford's. 6 a.m.

A book-lined first-floor room above a busy street in Covent Garden. It has a slightly shabby and pleasing atmosphere with a main entrance from a door R. *A window* L, *with venetian blinds, overlooks the (audible but unseen) street and a door far* L *leads to a small executive bathroom. The office contains Giles' cluttered desk and chair* UR *and Trish's desk with a word processor, etc., by the* R *door. There are book posters and a dartboard on the walls and a large clock is in a prominent position on one wall. Copies of Font Cairns' latest thriller — "Brains on Toast" — are piled around a life-sized cut-out of Cairns in front of Giles' desk. A photocopier stands far* L. *There is a carpet on the floor and drinks on a butler's tray*

When the CURTAIN *rises it is still quite dark but with city noises prowling and grumbling outside. The clock chimes six*

Monty, small and bearlike, is bumbling about amongst the furniture, humming a Sousa March, opening desk drawers and shining a torch inside — noseying about. He stops as its beam lights up the smug cardboard features of Font Cairns and he grunts dismissively, disgustedly. He moves to the bookshelves behind the cut-out figure and freezes as voices approach the door

Giles enters

Giles Thank God. Sanctuary. (*He goes to his desk and sits in the chair with his head in his hands*)

Jaffa enters and looks about

Monty peers over Cairns' shoulder, frowning

Jaffa So many books, eh. Publishing is a gentleman's profession of course ... (*He walks to the window and partly opens the blinds*)

Giles flinches

How is the hangover?

Giles Impending; when it starts I hope I die.

Jaffa You are a lucky man, my friend. You deal with the civilized creatures who create books; I struggle with animals, eh? Sharks, monkeys with money.

Giles You'd call those two tonight civilized?

Jaffa (*taking an orange from his pocket and toying with it*) Americans are natural gamblers, Giles, it is part of their culture — and poker is their natural game: ugly, direct, brutal, without irony or finesse. (*He smiles across the desk at Giles*) Is no game for English Gentleman.

Giles Hava — what have I done? (*He stares at Jaffa in horror*)

Jaffa I tried to stop you more than once. Is true old English saying, eh: "Lucky in love no damn luck at all in cards". Is true, Giles.

Giles Where did you learn to play like that? You destroyed the three of us.

Jaffa (*moving* C, *tossing the orange*) In a hard school.

Giles L.A. With the Mafia hoods?

Jaffa (*tossing, catching*) Matthausen, with the Guards actually.

Giles stares at him. Jaffa looks around

Speaking of them, don't you have any night security here?

Giles (*wearily*) Oh there's this indelibly boring old buffer somewhere around. Asleep in the basement probably ... (*He stares about*) Not that there's anything worth taking — just a load of books. (*His eyes come to rest on Font Cairns. He groans*)

Jaffa Hangover blossoming, eh?

Giles Just remembered, I've got to lunch *that* today — Font Cairns.

Jaffa Ah yes, the famous thriller writer.

Giles Famous pain in the backside ——

Jaffa Yes, I hear that too.

Monty Inedibly boring old buffer am I, Mr Short.

Giles (*starting up*) Good God it spoke!

Jaffa stops tossing the orange. Monty shuffles sideways into view, downcast but unfazed

Monty Surprised to hear you call me them names, Mr Short. It's me mentabolism for one thing, and for another — as I believe you know — I was starved for several years in a German Quarry near München Gladbach, n'cetera. (*He thinks*) N'cetera.

Giles Monty what are you doing in here?

Monty Just come on duty, haven' I. In my capacity as Security stroke Doorman first fing I does upon taking over from Rommel to uvver bloke is to check rahnd, n'cetera. (*To Jaffa*) Twenny years I bin checking rahnd this building, sah, and I don't fink we lost a paper clip in all that time.

Jaffa Twenty years. You must have met with some strange goings on?

Monty No sah, noffing. (*He sighs*) Not a break-in, not a bit of hanky-panky — noffing — in twenny years. Mind you when you bin through what I have you're ready for plenny of noffing, n'cetera ... (*He stops*) You're foreign intcha?

Giles Mr Hava Jaffa is a businessman, Monty ——

Monty (*noticing the orange*) Looks like the man from Del Monte — to Monty! (*He wheezes and gasps with mirth*) Polish?

Giles Monty ——

Jaffa Czech, actually.

Monty I met some Czechs when I was in the quarry — POW — breaking stones for Hitler's roads, n'cetera, living on swedes and black bleedin' bread, n'cetera. Czechs — they'd nick your laces out your boots while you was asleep ——

Giles I wonder if you'd be good enough to bring two very strong coffees.

Monty Inedibly boring old buffer's handy for summing then.

Giles shrugs apologetically. Monty shuffles to the door, pauses

Wiv' milk and sugar, n'cetera, n'cetera?

Jaffa No coffee for me, thank you, I must go in a moment.

Giles No milk, no sugar — thank you.

Monty Erarse, that's what we used to get in the quarry, nearly as bad as this stuff out the machine. Erarse, that's what they called it — we called it summing else. Bladdy gnats'piss weren't in it — well, maybe it was ... (*He sighs*) Erarse coffee, swedes, black bleedin' bread, n'cetera, n'cetera.

He exits, trailing "n'ceteras"

Jaffa puts his orange away

Jaffa Old English Soldier, eh — grand old Cockney Sparrer?

Giles He's the most boring man in the firm — if not the country. (*He thinks*) If not the world.

Jaffa chuckles

I'm not joking — ten minutes in the lift with him takes ten years off your life. People stagger up two flights of stairs to avoid him. (*He groans and rubs his temples*)

Jaffa Sure you wouldn't rather go home, Giles, I get my gorilla to run you?

Giles (*hit*) Home. No thanks, Hava. (*He comes around the desk to Jaffa*) I'd rather not face Verity just yet.

Jaffa Courage, *mon brave*, all is not yet lost, eh?

Giles (*forcing a wan smile*) Whatever the outcome — thank you.

Jaffa (*shrugging*) No-one believes this, but I am not interested in money. What is money? (*He wanders across to the window and stares down into the now-stirring street*) I know I should ask that of those awaking in doorways, eh, in cardboard boxes? But a man can only eat one meal at a time, make love to one woman; that beautiful motor car of mine down there can only convey me to Mayfair or somewhere else — not to paradise, eh? (*He moves back to Giles and runs his fingers behind Giles' suit lapels in an easy fondling gesture*) I admire your English phlegm, eh? To lose so bravely, to be so hurt and yet maintain the dignity.

Giles (*wryly*) Oh that's us all right — cricket, football, tennis, you name it we lose gamely at it.

They shake hands

Jaffa (*sombrely*) At least you play by the rules, eh, and without rules is no game at all — is soon barbarism. (*He smiles*) Good luck, Giles my friend, no confiding, eh?

Giles I said, I must explain to my wife — please?

Jaffa (*after a pause*) Her only, then.

Monty peers through the door, puffing, holding a plastic cup of coffee

Jaffa heads for the door

No fibbing, eh!

Giles No fibbing.

Jaffa goes out passing Monty with a mock salute

Monty almost salutes back with his coffee-bearing arm but stops himself and shuffles up to Giles

Monty One black coffee, Mr Short, wiv' no n'ceteras.

Giles Thank you, Monty. (*He takes the cup and walks to the window*)

Monty watches

Monty (*mysteriously*) Comes to us all, eh Mr Short?

Giles stares back at him

Comes to us all one fine day, n'cetera.

Giles The, er — reckoning?

Monty (*pleased*) Could call it that. My old muvver, Gawd bless her, she used to say: "There's always another day, Monty" when I was in a hurry, n'cetera, wanting summing she hadn't got, n'cetera — didn't wanna come in orff the streets, n'cetera, sort of fing. "There's always anuvver day", she used to say.

Giles stares out at the lightening sky

Giles Very wise.

Monty But there comes a day when there ain't always anuvver day, Mr Short — there comes a day when days is getting short, scarce, *rare.* Comes a morning ...

He realizes Giles isn't listening and heads for the door

When there ain't gonna be any more bleedin' mornings ... (*He stops. Barking at Giles' back*) Writer is he, that bloke wiv the orange?

Giles turns. Monty nods at Cairns' cut-out

One o' them?

Giles No he's — entrepreneur, bookmaker, casino owner — immensely wealthy, came over here after the War. (*Pause*) A rather strange and unpredictable, but brilliant, man.

Monty What's the orange for?

Giles No-one knows. He always carries one ...

Monty Well, Czech — you can expect anyfing, can't yer. (*Heading for the door; grumbling*) Poles, Czechs, Ukrainians, n'cetera. Polygon masses, n'cetera, you can expect the bleedin' worst.

Monty exits

Giles stands C, with his coffee, listening to the city coming to life outside

(*Murmuring*) God! What have I done?

Black-out

SCENE 2

The same. 9 a.m.

The Lights come up with the street bustling outside

Giles emerges from the bathroom in a clean shirt, tying on another tie. He sits at his desk

Trish enters and stares at him in surprise

Trish Oh! Good-morning, Mr Short.
Giles (*pleased to see her*) Morning, Trish.

He watches her trip towards the window

You're like a breath of sanity — a breath of the real, sensible world.
Trish (*hanging up her jacket, etc.*) You look awful, Mr Short.
Giles Thank you, Trish.
Trish I'll get you some fresh orange and an Anadin maximum strength. My gran swears by them — (*she giggles*) — says she'd be dead by now without them, so I say I'm going to hide them one day! She does laugh!
Giles How is your gran?
Trish Crabby, I think you'd call it. The doctor called the other day and gave her a check up. "How are you feeling, my dear?" he asked like he was talking to a brain damaged newt. "There's nothing wrong with me that a night with Tom Cruise wouldn't put right," she said! She does make me laugh. (*She giggles and heads for the door*) I mean, she's only eighty-five!

She exits then squeals just as if goosed by someone. Adrian Smethers sticks his red-bespectacled face around the door

Adrian (*like Eamonn Andrews*) Goiles Short. You tort you were in for another normal boring day at the office, didn't you ...?
Giles Hallo, Adrian.
Adrian But, Goiles Short, Fiction Editor and all round noice guy — this is your loife!

Adrian swaggers into the office and perches on a corner of the desk. Giles suffers him

So, how went the authors' bingey-poo?

Giles Desperate.

Adrian (*peering at him*) Mm, do you feel as bad as you look?

Giles Want a list? I've got a breezeblock rolling about inside my head, my heart's beating too fast, my tongue's turned to coconut matting, my haemorrhoids are killing me ——

Adrian sticks up his hands

Adrian All right! (*Peering again*) And I'd shut your eyes or you might bleed to death.

Giles How's yourself?

Adrian Just terrific.

Giles And Melissa and the Embryo?

Adrian Just wonderful, God she's big — she's colossal. (*Holding his hands in front of his belly*) you could put a window-box on it! (*He laughs*) OTT, yah? But I love her so much — and him ——

Giles stares

— that's what I came to tell you: she's had the scan, we've got a son!

Giles (*oddly subdued*) I'm glad for you.

Adrian (*beaming*) We're ecstatic about it.

Adrian strolls up to Cairns' cut-out and taps the title "Brains on Toast"

This is zooming up the lists I see. Haven't you got a meet with the great man today?

Giles For my sins. If he tells me his anecdote about Aleister Crowley one more time I think I'll puke.

Adrian Say what you like about him — he's number three for the fifth week running.

Giles He can write like I can do brain surgery, not that I've read one of his damn books right through.

Adrian (*shocked*) You're joking? Your top client ——

Giles What are publishers' readers for?

Adrian regards him, seriously for a change

Adrian What's the matter?

Giles Nothing ... (*He checks*) Well, I might as well start with you. Last night I lost my home, my car, about 35K — and almost certainly my wife when she finds out.

Adrian (*grinning*) Wha-at?

Giles (*in an affected voice*) My hice, Adrian. The superb late Georgian town hice with entrance hall, study, dining-room, family-room, master bedroom plus three, staff accomodation, mature gardens back and front, double garage — with a particularly attractive feature being the eighteenth-century panelling in the first-floor rooms. (*Normal voice*) All of which Verity adores!

Adrian Steady on, you *cannot* be serious!

Giles Everything I say is true ...

Adrian Nah! I've seen you like this before when you've been out with writers, it's called Alcoholic Remorse.

Giles gets up and strolls to the window

Writers and booze, it's a lethal combination. It's all right for them, of course — indulging in childish behaviour seems to be part of the creative process — but not you, Giles, not us.

Giles I'm ruined. (*Starting out*) I ought to be feeling suicidal, and I do a bit, but I also feel like — one in a million, you know?

Adrian No, I don't ...

Giles (*musing*) A changed cell in the vast comatose body of humanity — awakened. Any exhilarated ——

Adrian You're still pissed, right.

Trish enters with orange juice and Anadin

They watch her put them on Giles' desk and trip gracefully across the room to her desk

Adrian Wish I had such a lovely handmaiden.

Trish stops and smiles at them

I've been married almost four years now, Trish — can we have an affair?

Trish loses her smile

I've been told I'm extremely tasty in bed?

Trish (*tartly*) Who by — a bunch of fleas? Is there anything else, Mr Short?

Giles, grinning, shakes his head. Trish looks at Giles

Don't forget you're taking Mr Cairns to lunch? I've booked a table at Giovanni's.

Giles nods sombrely

And there's Monty's presentation.

Giles stares, puzzled

The liftman? He's retiring today. We had a whip-round, remember — you gave £20?
Giles Worth every penny. Thanks, Trish — wheel him in around three o'clock.

Trish turns to the computer. The phone rings on Giles' desk and Adrian picks it up

Adrian Rutherford's. ... Yes he is — just. It's Frances Feldman for you. (*He delays handing the phone to Giles; with his hand over the mouthpiece*) On the subject of having affairs, there's a long standing rumour she's your bit on the side?
Giles I detest that expression. Frances is one of our best readers.
Adrian And what else, eh? Nudge nudge, wink wink, say no more?
Giles My mistress — now if you'll excuse me.

He holds his hand out and Adrian gives him the phone

Hallo Fran, just Adrian mucking about ...

Adrian goes to door, grinning, not taking it seriously, looking at Trish

Adrian He must think we just got off the boat, eh! Mistress indeed ...

Adrian goes out, laughing

Trish takes some papers to Giles' desk and stands staring as Giles speaks into the phone

Giles Yes I do, Fran, you know I do — I'm not distant at all — had a rather grim night that's all. I swear I do. ... Well, we met Hava Jaffa, yes. ... A lot, Fran — in fact I've done something pretty stupid even for me — I mean sort of irrevocable maybe. ... Yes I am serious. We must talk about it. ... Yes, I'm afraid it could be the end of the world — as we know it anyway. ... ASAP, I think — no I've got a lunch appointment. ... Yes, Fran — bye for now.

He puts the receiver down and sees Trish's worried, puzzled expression and smiles wanly. She puts the file in front of him then sways gracefully across to the copier. Giles watches her start to operate the machine, stooping, pressing buttons

The Lights dim to denote the passing of time then come up again to 10.00 am brightness

Giles is still seated at the desk watching her but with Ray-Bans on. She senses his gaze and smiles shyly across room at him

Trish Feeling better, Mr Short?
Giles Slightly more human, thank you.

Pause. She puts more paper in the machine. Giles is in a kind of sunstruck reverie

> *Fergus peers shortsightedly around the door,* The Times *and briefcase in his hand*

Fergus Morning, all.
Giles Fergus.
Trish Morning, Mr Rutherford.

Fergus comes in and stops in front of the cut-out

Fergus Font? You here already? Nothing wrong I hope? (*He sticks out a hand and it bumps against the cardboard. He laughs*) Hell's flames! I thought it was him.
Giles If only. I wouldn't mind taking that to lunch.
Fergus Now Giles, that's just the kind of flip remark I wanted to warn you about: treat Font extra carefully today, will you? The bliddy poachers are after him a big way — (*angry*) in a blatant way — phoning him with outright offers, would you believe? I mean there was a time when publishers had ethics!
Giles (*mildly*) About the time of the Gutenberg Press?
Fergus (*looking myopically and sadly along the book titles on the shelves*) Rutherford's. A small but very distinguished firm publishing Archaeology, Art, Belles-lettres, Biographies, Memoirs, Novels — and now (*bumping into a pile of "Brains on Toast"*) sex and gore thrillers by the likes of ... (*He stumps back to the desk*) I think I'm getting too old for this game.
Giles Snap.

Fergus (*snapping out of it*) Anyway, be milk and honey to the old ... (*He stops and waves his fingers about*)

Giles Yes, Fergus.

Fergus We all know he's a pain in the ... (*He shakes his fingers again*)

Giles Yes, Fergus.

Fergus But he is also a phenomenal word machine. (*Tapping the cut-out words: "Brains on Toast"*) This will be top of the lists next week — we're setting up for a second reprint — d'you read me, Giles?

Giles I'll do my best.

Fergus Cherish him.

Giles You could lunch him yourself? I'm sure he'd be impressed.

Fergus (*hurriedly*) Afraid I've got someone else lined up: young poet from Fife, rather charming lassie — and good ... (*Heading for the door*) I'll love you and leave you then.

Fergus goes out

Giles smiles ruefully at Trish

Trish Nice try, Mr Short.

Fergus pops back

Fergus Just bear in mind what a major asset Cairns is.

Fergus goes again

Giles (*murmuring*) Major ass — something, definitely.

He takes the Ray-Bans off and falls to watching Trish again as she works on the copier, bending over it to adjust a lever. She straightens and looks across at him

Trish What are you thinking, Mr Short?

Giles (*without thinking*) Trish. You are a lovely young woman and I'd like to get up and kiss you breathless then bend you over the copier in a desperate and unusual act of love — since you asked.

Trish (*giggling*) Mr Short!

Giles Not very PC I know but every time you use the copier I desire something like that — variations on an erotic theme.

Trish I'd no idea! (*She giggles*) So what stops you?

Giles (*sighing*) The obvious I suppose. I know you have your aged grandmother in Pinner; a young man, no doubt.

Trish shakes her head

Or a fiancé even.

Trish shakes her head again, smiling

Nobody?

Trish Nobody serious.

Giles Anyway, I don't want to hurt you or ruin your life by toying with your feelings — and mine's complicated enough to be honest.

Trish (*sadly*) Oh.

Giles I do respect and like you very much as a person and a colleague, of course.

Trish (*dreamily*) "Desperate and unusual act of love" — never heard it called that before.

Pause

How unusual?

Giles Oh, use your imagination.

Trish thinks

Trish (*after a pause*) That *is* unusual.

Giles I hope I haven't offended you, You did ask ...

Trish (*walking back to her desk*) Of course not, Mr Short — and it's ditto about the respect and liking.

She sits at her desk and starts to sort out the copies. Giles finds himself staring at her back, her nape

Verity enters with two expensive shopping bags which she dumps before going up to his desk for a kiss and a hug

Verity I've been worried about you.

Giles I told you I was entertaining clients — Americans, on the town? You know what that's like.

Verity I looked in the spare room and the bed was empty. Did you have a dreadful time Gilesy-Wilesy? (*Stroking his face*) You look ravaged.

Giles disentangles himself from her arms

Giles (*conducting her to a chair and sitting her down*) Verity, please sit, there's something I must try to explain.

Verity I'm meeting Mummy for lunch, darling, I hope it isn't one of your
  lectures about household economy ——
Giles *Please* ...

*Verity subsides into the chair in front of the desk like a chastened little girl
and stares wide-eyed at Giles*

Verity Is Daddy cwoss?
Giles No, Daddy is not cwoss — cross — but he's afraid Mummy is going
  to be, you see last night I ——
Verity (*cutting in*) I must tell you! I've just had *the most* torrid session on
  the phone with Liz. She and Mark have absolutely come apart this time:
  he's gone off to Wales in a fearful huff and poor Liz is determined not to
  have him back. (*A fierce whisper*) The *Lebanese male au pair* — what did
  I tell you?
Giles I took Hank and Wilbur to the Orange Club and Jaffa was there.

Verity sobers as if drenched in cold water

Verity Not Hava Jaffa.

Giles nods. Verity sighs

  You lost, of course.

He nods. She sighs. Trish listens

  Darling, why don't you learn: you are not lucky; you are not the gambling
  type. Did you lose heavily?
Giles Like a lord.
Verity That man is evil!
Giles (*pondering*) No, not evil, bad possibly — a crook no doubt, but with
  a strange code of honour, a sporting streak.
Verity Now much?
Giles I lost about 30K and signed a cheque for a serious amount more ——

Verity gapes

  — then it was the Jag, I'm afraid, then the rosewood secretaire in the
  drawing-room ——

Verity gasps

  — seems he's had his eye on it since he came to dinner that time.

Verity Mummy gave us that! Giles, this isn't funny ——
Giles Not funny at all, though it seemed hilarious and tragic at the time. I was in a trance — *relinquishing* things.
Verity I sometimes think you've been in a trance all your life!

Trish approaches Giles' desk with a folder then stops as she senses tension

Trish Oh I'm sorry.
Giles What is it, Trish?
Trish Just the late morning mail — and a couple of readers' reports.
Giles Thank you.

Trish slips the folder into the tray in front of Verity and smiles shyly at her

Trish Hallo, Mrs Short.

Verity gives a perfunctory smile and notices Giles watching Trish sway gracefully to the exit

   Trish goes

Verity Trish — who would give a child a name like that?
Giles Her parents presumably.
Verity (*waspishly condescending*) Trish: change the "i" to an "a" and the poor thing's garbage.

Giles watches Verity idly pick up the folder and open it. One reader's report has a mauve envelope marked "Giles" clipped to it. Verity sniffs it

Verity What dreadfully butch cologne. (*She frowns*) Smells familiar. (*Reading the envelope*) "Giles" — who is it from?
Giles Afraid the old x-ray vision isn't working too well this morning. (*Suddenly edgy*) Put it down, Verity.
Verity Is it from your bit of fluff, darling?
Giles (*laughing too readily*) What a quaint old expression — "bit of fluff" — it's from one of our readers, since it *was* attached to her report.
Verity A billet-doux. (*Half teasing, half serious*) Well at least it isn't from a man.
Giles I have a bet with Hava Jaffa ——
Verity (*still toying with the envelope*) It doesn't matter, darling, I'm sure you'll sort it out as usual.
Giles I bet the house and everything.
Verity (*laughing*) You're still drunk!

Giles Wish I was. (*He glances at the window*) I sometimes think I'd like to stay drunk forever — wandering around the streets with an ever-lasting bottle of Smirnoff in the pocket of a disgusting mac.

Verity (*gathering up her bags*) I'm meeting Mummy at Harvey Nicks, darling.

Giles (*gently*) Our beautiful home, I'm so sorry ... I've *lost* it.

Verity stares at him and sees he's telling the truth and slumps back into the chair

Verity What — happened?

Giles Even the Yanks were broke when we left the table, expertly skinned by Jaffa. I knew there was no question of withdrawal — you just don't renege at that level. We stood in that cavernous hallway of his and I found myself staring at his hands — he's got hands like a navvy, you know? But gone soft from high living: plump fingers with heavy gold rings on, rather vulgar but worth a fortune.

Verity To hell with his hands! If this isn't some sick joke you've cooked up you must talk to him, or Daddy's solicitor ——

Giles He's a remarkable man, gambling is his life, they say — and his honour. They say he'll bet on two raindrops running down a window — which reaches the sill first?

Verity You men are insane! Honour? You stand there and tell me you wagered a house worth a million and a half on the open market to that — mittel-European *bookie*! No, Giles!

Giles I'd lost everything else, my brain was racing as we shook hands on the step — how could I drag something back? I sensed there was another trick to be played; I sensed he was enjoying himself, toying with me. Then it came to me, a mad wild card, desperate last gasp idea that might just appeal to his strange Slavic mentality.

Verity (*gathering the bags, getting up*) Don't tell me! I feel like a baglady, damn you! I don't want to know, just sort it out.

She heads for the door, then turns

I will not be socially humiliated, Giles — don't come home until everything's all right again — *I mean it!*

Giles (*mildly, regretfully*) Verity. I do wish you'd produce another reaction to life's occasional unpleasantness ——

Verity Unpleasantness? What would you call an atomic bomb going off in Fortnum's: a bit of a *faux pas*?

Giles Jaffa's right, he said: "The English are closer to the Oriental than the European — they hate to lose face."

Verity I don't care what Hava Jaffa said! (*She comes back to front of desk, glaring*) I can't believe you'd be so irresponsible! Why did you do it?

Giles Jaffa. I turned to him and those liquorice black eyes of his seemed to look right into my mind, daring me. He's a ridiculous Anglophile you know, longs to be an English gentleman and all that — I'm amazed he still thinks they exist after 1500 years of Tory Government.

Verity Sod your politics! Mummy was right about you ——

Giles (*interrupting*) "There's something else," I said, "I know the cards are cold now but we could have a gentleman's wager?" "Vat can you put up?" he asked like a fat vampire, as if he already knew. I said: "The last thing I have apart from my capacity for love and my soul ..."

He stops as Verity picks up the envelope again and, almost absently, tears it open

What are you doing?

Verity I have smelt that cologne before. (*She opens the note. Reading*) "My dearest G. I know this is strictly *verboten* but I just had to say *Knicker Elastic* is wonderful — (*she flickers a look at Giles*) — extremely tight, gripping". *Knicker Elastic*?

Giles A first novel, (*rummaging amongst the scripts, etc., on the desk*) got a copy here somewhere ... Young writer, all fantasy of course, bit like early Martin Amis — with a dash of *Portnoy's Complaint* ...

Verity (*reading*) "You must buy it. Yours in profound love, my all-darkness — F.F." Who is she, Giles?

Giles One of our best readers.

Verity (*crumpling up the note and throwing it at him*) How long!

Giles Been on our books about ten years on and off ——

Verity Mostly on by the sound of it! I mean how long have you been screwing?

Giles (*sighing*) Er — Christmas '83.

Verity (*shattered*) My godfathers. That was only three years after our marriage ...

Giles (*musing*) I took a novel for her to try out — it was snowing and my feet got wet.

Verity (*seething*) What was it called: "Drop your drawers it's Santa Claus"?

Giles She insisted that I take off my socks ——

Verity Is that what F.F. stands for: Foot Fetishist?

Giles Verity ——

Verity Or is it Fantastic Foreplay! Or Furtive Fornication! (*She looks at the note again*) "My *all-darkness*": does she really call you that? Yerch! Who is she!

Giles (*sadly*) Frances Feldman.

Verity (*shocked rigid*) No. Not Fran — tell me it isn't true, Giles, please ... (*Madly inspired*) It's some, some ... it's the bet you were talking about, isn't it! You swine! You bet Jaffa you could convince me you'd been having an affair all these years — that's it, isn't it?

Giles No.

Verity (*taking it on the chin*) No.

Giles I'm so sorry, I'd have carried it to the grave rather than tell you — in the normal run of things.

Verity Well thank you very much! (*She thinks*) God, I think I recommended her to you!

Giles What Fran and I have had together was never meant to touch you; I value our good marriage ——

Verity (*dazed*) Yes, a good marriage! I've always thought so, our friends have always thought so. Frances Feldman is one of my best friends! The bitch!

She backs towards the door with her bags

Trish enters

Don't come back to the house, you bastard! Half of it is mine — you were wrong to gamble with my half.

Giles I don't want to lose you; why did you have to open the letter?

Verity Why tell me the truth, you cruel, betraying, philandering swine! Why the sudden rush of honesty from genitals to brain!

Giles That's the bet.

Verity That you could smash my life to smithereens in ten minutes?

Giles Jaffa. I offered him, on my honour — winner takes all — that I'd tell the truth for a day.

Pause. They stare at each other. Trish, at the door, watches them

The truth, the whole truth, et cetera — God, I'm getting Monty's disease. If and when asked, without prevarication, straight out with the unvarnished whatsit, regardless of cost, for twelve hours.

Verity You're mad, both of you are barking ——

Giles It was all I had left, my integrity.

Verity (*close to hysteria*) Integrity? You've just admitted to having had a rampant bloody mistress for over ten years and you've got *integrity*!

Giles A few tattered shreds ——

Verity Thank God we never had children — I'm so glad I never gave into you about that.

Giles (*slightly pained*) No, you made it quite clear from the off: "Oh the mess, darling, the awful shitty chaos of breeding — and isn't the world teeming with unwanted brats already?"

Verity You agreed! You said: "I'm about as interested in children as I am in learning to play the Peruvian nose-flute"!

Giles stares, remembering

How could you do this to me? (*As it sinks in*) What will Liz and Mark say? And Julian and Vanessa, Peter and Charles and Margo — dear God.

Giles (*drily*) Yes, I'm afraid we're going to be crossed off more dinner lists than Hannibal Lecter unless ——

Verity Fran Feldman of all people! She knows me inside out, dammit, I've told that woman things I ... (*She stops, horrified*)

Giles If I can survive until 6 p.m. without lying they'll never know — all will be restored.

Verity She could go on bloody *Mastermind* with what she knows about us. "Oh yes, Magnus, I'm an authority on the Shorts — I know all their goings and comings and" ... (*She stops again, hand over mouth in horrified recollection*) Everything.

Giles If I don't fib there'll be no harm done.

Verity No harm done? You bloody fool, Giles! I'll never forgive you for this!

She goes out ignoring Trish

Giles sits down and holds his head in his hands. Trish is about to close door

Monty ambles in

Monty *Arrivederci*, n'cetera. People rushin' abaht like blue-arsed flies today — it's bleedin' *chaa*-otic,

Giles (*wearily*) What do you want, Monty?

Monty goes up to the desk with Trish following him

Monty Toylits, Mr Short, *hue*rinals, great white telephones in the floor, bogs, n'cetera — *and* toylit paper for the use of?

Giles shakes his head

I mean, I know there's a bleedin' recession, n'cetera, but nicking toylit paper? I dunno what the bleedin' world's coming to.

Giles Incredible.

Monty That's what I said on the way here, Mr Short — hincredible I said — so I bin sitting in there waiting for the culprit, see? Listening for the sound of rolls coming off holders, n'cetera, straining me lugholes, n'cetera, and doing me piles no good at all.

Giles Your devotion to duty humbles me ——

Monty Got 'em in the quarry near München Gladbach, o' course, sitting on them granite rocks. Like ruddy boulders, they are.

He stops as Trish takes his arm, smiling beguilingly, steering him to the door

Trish Come and talk to me about it, eh? Mr Short's got other things to think about right now.

Monty Aw — right. (*He grins and winks at Giles*) Be seeing you later on anyway, Mr Short for the old (*he mimes passing something to someone*) pressie passover, n'cetera?

Trish ushers him out, glancing back at Giles who yanks an imaginary toilet chain

Trish giggles and closes the door on herself and Monty

Giles strolls to the window and opens it, letting in the bustle from the street below. He listens and watches the streetlife for a moment then goes back to his desk and takes a set of darts from a drawer. He stands before the board, takes aim and lets fly one, two, three darts, and walks to collect them from the board. On the way back from the board he looks more relaxed, soothed by the game. He takes aim again and can't let go of the dart and stands on the oche with his loaded arm pecking back and forth and dismay on his face

Black-out

SCENE 3

The same. 11.30 a.m.

The Lights come up on Trish working at her desk. Giles at his desk is signing letters quickly. Font Cairns lounges near his cardboard clone nursing a gin and tonic and boring fruitily on. The drinks tray is nearby with bottles, ice, soda syphon, etc.

Cairns ... So there I was, a sleepy pretty child in my little nightgown clasping my father's hand as he walked me to the head of that long dining-table. And there *he* sat, the guest of honour, the great beast himself — Crowley. And as he swung his head to look at me — still chewing his food with enormous deliberation, like some kind of ruminating animal — I felt an emanation of cold and obdurate evil. A sense of utter boredom, too, Giles?

Giles Mm, Monty gives me that feeling. Sorry to keep you waiting, Font.

Cairns Absolutely my fault, dear boy. I decided to call for you on impulse. I hate waiting in restaurants these days — *starers*, you know?

Giles Really?

Cairns My dear boy, since *The South Bank Show* I can scarcely shop without being — ogled.

Giles Well, should be OK in Giovanni's.

Cairns We're going there again? I hear Hutchinsons do their scribes at Le Gavroche.

Giles Yes, I heard that.

Cairns Oh well, one osso bucco is more or less like another. (*He picks up a copy of "Brains on Toast" and fondles it*) Did you read what Branwell said in the *Observer* about this? "Cairns' prose hisses and crackles about the mind for days after reading it." Wasn't that sweet of him?

Giles You're back together again? Last time we met you said you wouldn't put him out if he was being flambé'd on a trolley before your very eyes.

Cairns (*sighing*) It's a marriage, dear boy — you know what they're like; awfully narrow and constricting but compelling for that reason — and better than being alone — just.

Giles smiles

I have to have someone to take care of the trivia while I write; I need my cocoon of caring domesticity, you know?

Giles I understand that.

Cairns (*touring the room with his book*) "Hisses and crackles around the mind". (*Pause*) Did you feel that, dear boy?

Giles (*after a pause, carefully*) Not exactly.

Cairns (*oblivious*) Still gives me a kick, y' know Giles, to think that I give so many people — strangers, foreigners — so much pleasure through my work. One must never become blasé, dear boy: keep the responses keen, listen, take note, observe — reflect inwardly and regurgitate when the time is right, isn't that our craft, dear boy?

Giles Yes, sickening, isn't it.

Cairns Still knocking the odd poem out, I trust?

Giles (*sweetly*) Yes, I'm trying to get enough rejection slips to wallpaper the bathroom.

Cairns Feeling a bit off colour, dear boy?

Giles (*shrugging*) Something and nothing, forgive me. (*He closes the file of letters and stands up*) Right, shall we proceed?

They head for the door together

Fergus strides in

Fergus Font! I heard you were in the building, dear chap.
Cairns Fergus.

Fergus embraces the cut-out then looks at them and laughs as if it was deliberate. They laugh dutifully

Fergus Lord, man, you're a shadow of your former self! (*He embraces the real Cairns, patting his back*) Wonderful book, your best ever!

Cairns laps this up modestly

Could *not* put the thing down — didn't you find that, Giles?

Giles wriggles for a moment and is about to speak

Cairns Oh, Giles doesn't enthuse — he's very undemonstrative, aren't you, dear boy? One might almost say taciturn.
Fergus Och he's English, Font, and southern English come to that. He hasn't the mad Celtic influence we have. (*He glares at Giles behind Cairns' back*)
Cairns No. (*Regarding Giles*) He's very neat, isn't he. You do occupy space very *neatly*, Giles.
Giles Thanks.
Cairns Truth's truth, lovely — (*irritated by Giles*) you're the kind of average, comfortably off, plain chappie one sees a dozen times on a short Tube journey. Everyman, that's you in a nutshell.
Giles Now I am depressed. (*He checks his watch*) Shall we?
Cairns A thumbnail sketch, of course. You're a bit of a chameleon, aren't you — you merge with your surroundings.
Giles God. (*He sighs*) I'm going down and down in my estimation.
Fergus You must be delighted with the progress of "Brains on Toast". It has taken off like a rocket.
Cairns Mm, I'll be happier when I get out of that pen-scribbling woman's fat backside and show her mine! I love to topple those feisty intellectual bitches, y'know — they hate my work, the menopausal old milch cows!

Giles stares. Cairns calms himself. Fergus hugs him again then shakes hands

Fergus Grand to see you but I must be off! Have a marvellous lunch, you two!

He gives Giles a pointed look and exits with a Gaelic cry equivalent to "bon appetit"

Cairns seems reluctant to put his book down. Giles checks his watch again

Giles Well ...
Cairns (*at* c)Tell me, Giles, what *do* you think of this? (*He sticks the book under his nose*) I know I can trust you to be frank; one meets so many envious bitches and sycophants, and it really has drained me somewhat, this one. (*He strokes the book*) Seven months' hard labour and a difficult birth but, as Fergus so kindly remarked, my best — I do believe.

He smirks at Giles who wriggles like a pinned butterfly before him. Trish turns to watch

Be candid, dear boy, refresh me with your honest appraisal?
Trish Your table's booked for twelve, Mr Short.
Giles (*grasping this*) Yes! Shall we discuss ——
Cairns No prevarication, dear boy, tell me!
Giles To be honest, Font, and I feel I owe you that, I haven't finished reading it — yet.

Cairns emits a pained caw of disbelief

Cairns You haven't *finished it yet*? You're pulling my leg.
Giles No, sorry.
Cairns Eye trouble?

Giles shakes his head

Then why?
Giles I — er — found it rather hard going, I'm afraid.
Cairns Hard — going. You say "hard going" to one who prides himself upon being the most accessible of authors?
Giles (*sighing*) Can't we just say that "Brains on Toast" isn't my cup of tea and leave it at that.
Cairns (*glacial*) Is that intended to be funny? Am I to understand that you haven't read it *at all*?
Giles It was recommended by our most trusted reader ...

Watched raptly by Giles and Trish, Cairns paces the room as he speaks

Cairns This is staggering. I can't believe my ears. What kind of editor doesn't read what is practically the only best seller on his list! Why doesn't he do that basic requirement?

Giles (*shrugging apologetically*) I'm afraid I jut don't seem to have a best-seller mind ——

Cairns (*stopping; whinnying*) Wha-aaat?

Giles I did try, I fell asleep with it several nights ——

Trish giggles with anxiety

Cairns (*brandishing the book in Giles' face*) So, it's a soporific if nothing else! I should have submitted it to Superdrug! Why didn't you put that in the publicity: Font Cairns' new thriller works better than Mogadon!

Giles I could tell after three pages it would be an enormous success, of course ——

Cairns (*hooting*) You managed three pages? (*Applauding*) Hooray!

Giles (*hopelessly*) A mega-success.

Cairns But not with Giles Short. I've always had a niggling suspicion that you regard my work as beneath you — as bad even?

Giles Can I refer my honourable friend to the answer I gave a few moments ago?

Cairns No! Answer me — do you think my books are bad?

Giles (*evenly*) I don't think there are good or bad books, Font, just well or badly written ones.

Trish watches in the background, between them, like a tennis spectator

Cairns So which category would you place mine in!

Giles (*sighing*) I regret to have to say: the latter.

Cairns How dare you! You mini minor poet! You little clerk! What have you ever written? A tissue of slight love poems, published by old Fergus because you're the nearest thing he has to a son! As an act of charity!

Giles muses aloud as Cairns twists to and fro before him, hopping mad

Giles Sad, isn't it. I've loved words all my life — and books until recently — treasured, hoarded, relished them, treated them like children, set them up and sent them toddling out into the cruel world. Most to sink without trace ——

Cairns Except mine, you nonentity!

Giles When they've done well I've been proud. Open a good book — I mean a well written book — and inhale the heady gust of ink and paper and latch on to the first sentence: a gate opens into another world.

Cairns You arty-farty swine! What's wrong with my worlds?

Giles (*mildly matter of fact*) "Brains on Toast", "Blood in the Barbie", "The Soil Sandwich"?

Cairns Yes!

Giles This is only my opinion, it may not be the objective truth but I find them worse than reality — seedy, sleazy, somehow unredeemed. Your researched bits are glaringly obvious, your effects are utterly cynical, and designed to appeal to the worst in your readers ——

Cairns Yes, my readers! There are countries with smaller populations! They adore me — they are avid for my books — what about them?

Giles They have my pity. In my humble opinion "Brains on Toast" is a dirty, nasty book for a dirty, nasty world — only the world and some of its people deserve better. Your work doesn't enhance life, it smears and spoils it. It hates innocence, and women; it's Hank Janson with a dash of psychology and a modern glitz, (*he sighs*) and everyone in the business knows your hero is merely doing some of the things you fantasize about when dear old Branwell is playing with your ——

Cairns Your eyes have turned green, Giles Short! I know raging jealousy when I see it! What would you do if I threw this G and T in your face, you bitter, envious, miniature poetaster!?

Giles (*picking up the soda syphon; calmly*) I'd probably give you a soda shampoo.

Cairns You are nothing! I am lionized wherever I go, I've got a villa in Tuscany, a house in Morocco and an apartment in New York! My books sell by the shipload all over the globe! What d' you think of that?

Giles (*sadly*) All those trees that once felt the wind stirring their branches, all those leaves and buds and birds' nesting places turned into toilet paper for the mind — it does depress me.

Cairns (*turning about, book in one hand, drink in the other; shrill*) You closet poets are all the same: timid, bitter little failures going on about your love of words and slagging off *big writers* like me! You haven't got what it takes, that's the truth! You haven't the energy or the ideas! The lust for experience ... (*Casting his gin and tonic into Giles' face*) Oh take that! Bugger your poetry!

Trish gasps as Giles calmly steps close to Cairns with the soda syphon

(*Sneering*) *Just you dare ...*

Giles You take this, Font Cairns — or should I say Brian Sugget ——

Cairns winces

— for foisting your rotten vision on the world — bless you, old chap.

He squirts soda into Cairns' disbelieving face, then down his shirt front, and across it; then, pulling his waistband out, down his trousers inside, pressing until Cairns can stand no more, until soda runs from his turn-ups and he reels towards the door

(*Screaming*) You're finished, Short! You're stopped, Short! You're ruined! You won't get a job on the *Big Issue* when I'm through with you!

He yanks the door open and goes out

(*Off, shouting*) Fergus! Fergus where the hell are you?

Pause. Trish hands Giles a hankie or towel and watches him pat his face dry

Trish Not having a very nice day, are you?
Giles (*smiling*) I've had better. But it's strange, I feel terrified but excited too.
Trish You're terrifying me. Do you have to do this to yourself?
Giles What do you really want, Trish Evans?

She stares

At the end of the day? When your gran joins the majority, bless her, and your life's your own again? What would you wish your reward to be from a kind fate?
Trish Someone to love, of course.
Giles Simple as that.
Trish Someone who makes it all worthwhile.
Giles But how will you know it's really love, how will you know: *this is it*?
Trish You just do, I know I do — I mean, your heart just leaps when that person walks into the room.
Giles So you do have someone, Trish.
Trish Yes, Mr Short.
Giles And he walks into the room and your heart leaps and that's enough?
Trish Of course, what else is there?
Giles (*checking his watch suddenly*) Lunch at Giovanni's — if you'd like to?
Trish But — what about Mr Cairns?
Giles (*looking at the cut-out*) Yes, don't just stand there, Font. (*Picking it up*) Come along!

He heads for the door with the cut-out tucked under his arm. Trish grabs her jacket and dashes out after them, giggling

Black-out

SCENE 4

The same. 3 p.m.

The Lights come up on Fergus sitting at Giles' desk. The clock now shows 3 p.m.

Fergus (*on the phone*) Well, try again and keep trying — try his Moroccan number. If he's not there ... I know he's hardly had time to get to Morocco but try it anyway. ... Bugger the expense! If you do get hold of him tell him I implore him to get in touch with me. ... Yes — implore!

He puts the receiver down and it rings at once. He answers it

Fergus Rutherford speaking. ... No, he damn well is not. Who is this? ... Well I'm sorry, Mrs Feldman ... sorry, *Miss* Feldman ... sorry, *Ms* Feldman, I'd like to have words with him myself but he's no' here. ... At lunch apparently — with his secretary!

He slams the phone down. Pause. He drums his fingers on the desk. The phone rings again and he answers it

Rutherford. ... Och hallo, Verity. ... No, he's at lunch still. He was supposed to be with Font Cairns. ... My dear, I am as bewildered as you are, I don't know what has got into him. He's the most sensible, level-headed chap in the business, I agree. Has he been showing any signs of stress or ...

Giles enters, grinning, with one arm around the cardboard Cairns. He has the makings of a black eye and his tie is askew. Trish follows

Look, would you ring back? ... Thank you, dear girl. (*He puts the receiver down and regards Giles then nods towards the door*) Sure you've some work to do, Miss Evans?

Trish goes out

How did you get a face like that?

Giles Usual method, I gather. Mum and Dad got together one night and after that it was the luck of the genetic draw.

Fergus (*barking*) Don't be flip with me, laddie! What the hell happened?

Giles (*fondly putting the cut-out back in its place*) This yuppie at the next table started picking on my client. I know he wasn't saying much and refused to sit down but there was no reason to insult him.

Fergus What happened with the real Font Cairns!

Giles (*facing him*) He asked my honest opinion of his work.

Fergus So what happened to the essential fibulae? The old fibbing mechanism malfunctioned did it?

Giles I just can't lie today.

Fergus What's so special about today? Road to Damascus Day, is it — National Truth Day or what?

Giles I can't lie, it's as simple as that.

Fergus Good God, man, you're my Fiction Editor!

Giles Surely you're not suggesting that fiction is a form of lying ——

Fergus I'm suggesting you've lost us the flower of this House! Font Cairns may be an orchid flourishing on a pile of his own dung but he's practically keeping us solvent! His books ... Christ I don't have to tell you this ——

Giles The best fiction, far from being lies, has its own laws and truth, its own morality ——

Fergus Don't preach to me, Giles! I was buying books when you were delivering papers on your bike!

Giles Sorry.

Pause. Fergus calms down and studies Giles

Fergus There has to be a way round this. Let's examine this reckless outburst of honesty together. Have you been working too hard of late perhaps?

Giles shakes his head

Trouble at home? Surely not, your marriage has been a source of wonder and envy to us all for years. (*He thinks*) I know you've had the occasional wee (*he glances at the copier*) refresher, but we're both men of the world and no real harm done. What *is it*, my boy?

Giles I have to tell the truth for twelve hours or I'm ruined — damned.

Fergus (*gently, sadly*) With whom do you think you've made this covenant, my boy, is it the good Lord himself?

Giles I haven't flipped my lid. (*He thinks*) In fact, I've never felt so sane.

Fergus Who the hell are you to decide what the truth is anyway?

Giles As I see it, speaking as I find ——

Fergus So you've set yourself up as judge and critic of a man whose readership spans the globe, whose first book is in its tenth edition in Sierra Leone — God alone knows what they make of it — but, who are you to condemn all those teeming Font Cairns fans as morons?

Giles I haven't, it was my personal view ——

Fergus Sounds mighty like intellectual snobbery to me! You realize you've put in jeopardy the livelihood of everyone in this building? You can't go around telling the truth, man, especially not to authors — hell, you know what a bunch of sensitive egomaniacs they are. "Tell me the truth, give me your honest opinion", they bleat when what they really crave is the honey of unalloyed dripping praise! Tell a writer the truth and he'll take out a contract on you! (*He sobers again*) You've broken one of the cardinal rules of the business, Giles — I'm sorry.

Giles What does sorry mean, Fergus?

Fergus The phones have been red hot. If I can get to Font before the others do I might just be able to keep him on our list with an Amis-sized advance for his next book and a lot of arselicking — but I know he's going to demand something which hurts me far more.

Giles My head on a plate.

Fergus (*hit, nodding*) Tell me why you're doing this, son? Why are you so determined to self-destruct?

Giles I can't tell you, it's part of the deal.

Fergus Damn and hell's flames! The world's gone mad ... (*He calms himself with an effort*) Listen, when I do get hold of Font I'm going to fawn over him, I'm going to be so obsequious, nay emmolient, I'll probably hate myself for the rest of my life. But, I'm going to do anything short of sodomy to get him back here — and you are going to apologize to him, for all our sakes. Giles?

Giles picks up the set of darts and strolls to the oche and starts to play, engrossed in this familiar therapy

If you won't you can clear your desk! I mean it, hell's flames!

Fergus goes out leaving the door open

Giles gets the darts from the board and walks back to the oche

Melissa comes into the room and regards him with a hand across her proud belly

Giles Melissa.
Melissa Hallo, Giles.

He goes to her and stops a pace away, staring

Giles My God. I always think how on earth will the huge blighter get out —
I mean, you look so fecund, so great. I am in awe of you, Melissa.

Melissa I feel as though I'm being devoured by a parasite. D'you think it's
fun following this (*holding her belly*) around all day?

He stares, dashed

Adrian's told me about this truth nonsense ——

Trish enters looking worried

Trish (*seeing Melissa*) Oh sorry, Mr Short.

Giles It's OK, Trish, we're old friends.

Trish goes to the copier and starts to set it up. Melissa takes Giles DR

Melissa Giles.

Giles (*softly with conviction*) Don't *worry* ——

Adrian enters, excited, flushed

Adrian Sorry, darling.

Melissa Where did you go?

Adrian Monty grabbed me, something about bog paper bandits — I think
he's finally flipped. Giles, we were at lunch and the place started buzzing
— did you really drench him with soda?

Giles (*nodding*) I was severely provoked, m'lud.

*He throws darts into the board and goes to collect them with Adrian hopping
excitedly at his side. Giles continues throwing and collecting the darts during
the following*

Adrian I hear your job's on the line — I'm desperately sorry, old man.

Giles (*pulling darts from the board*) Are you? Or wasn't there a frisson of
something else when you heard: a sense of change, of things opening up
— possibilities?

Adrian No! I'm genuinely sorry, saddened, shocked — aren't we, darling?

Melissa (*eyes on Giles*) Yes — concerned too.

Giles Don't protest too much, Adrian, I know you've wanted Fiction Editor
for years.

Adrian Maybe. I'm as ambitious as the next man, but not like this —
honestly, Giles!

Giles Be careful, some words are Semtex ——

Trish Mr Short, you're not leaving?

Giles Don't worry, Adrian will look after you, won't you?

Adrian With pleasure.

Melissa gives Adrian a look

I really resent the inference that I'm pleased about this.

He follows Giles to the board to collect the darts again

I consider us friends, dammit, not just colleagues.

Giles Be honest then, friend?

Adrian I am — I always am!

Giles gives him a hard look

I often am! Good heavens I owe you: you picked me out of the ruck for kids'
books, I'll always be grateful.

Giles You're a good editor, I wish you well if you do get my desk.

Melissa You must stop this honesty binge, I mean people get murdered every
day for telling the truth — you've only got to read the tabloids: "Husband
kills wife in sex-taunt case then kills himself". It's one of the main causes
of violent death: informers telling on crooks, married men about their little
flings ...

Adrian It's crazy.

Trish (*approaching*) It is, Mr Short, listen to your friends.

Melissa What are you trying to prove?

Giles Nothing. But I'm finding out about myself in leaps and bounds.

Adrian You're dismantling yourself I'd say.

Giles So why do I feel — exalted — as well as terrified, guilty and miserable?
I feel as if I'm losing a skin of dirt each time I speak the truth. I see clean
flesh under the scabs.

Adrian What about those around you?

Melissa You've no right to hurt others.

Giles I don't think it's contagious.

Melissa But where will you draw the line?

Giles I don't know, until I'm asked.

Adrian (*almost whispering*) I gather this Jaffa's nothing but a criminal —
surely you don't have to honour a bet with a man like that? He's not *here*.

Giles goes to collect the darts once more

Melissa You could be asked anything.
Adrian About anybody.
Giles (*smiling mildly*) Get ye behind me, Adrian and Melissa. I gave him my
   word.

*Adrian and Melissa stare at each other then head for the door. Adrian exits
first, Melissa pauses in doorway, looking back at Giles, hard, then she goes
out*

Giles sighs and goes to his desk. He sees Trish staring at him

Trish She seems nice. Why does he have to be such a cleverdick?
Giles (*absently*) He's sterile.
Trish Wha-at? He thinks he's such a lady-killer!
Giles I shouldn't have told you — he swore me to secrecy.
Trish He told you?
Giles He had too much to drink one night — a crying drunk's confession.
   (*Shrugging*) Not his fault his sperms are as rare as penguins in the Kalahari
   — but he compensates, no man wants to be *unable* to father a child.
Trish (*glancing to the door*) She had treatment, I suppose.
Giles (*glancing towards the copier*) Yes.

He opens the drawer and starts to lifts things out

   The stuff one accumulates. Photos, postcards, bits and bobs ... Could you
   find me a couple of boxes, Trish?

*He looks up as she snuffles and sees that she's breaking up, dabbing her eyes
with a silly little hankie*

   You mustn't go soft on me, it's not the end of the world.
Trish (*crying now*) In a way it is. I'm sorry, Mr Short, but I've been so happy
   working for you. Our little jokes and routines, your many kindnesses:
   letting me get off early on Fridays and my hair done on lunchbreaks, always
   asking after my gran. I think *I* shall look for another position if you do leave!

Giles goes to her side

Giles Please don't do that. You've done so well here — a coveted and valued
   secretary. Promise me you don't throw it away?

Trish What will you *do*, Mr Short?
Giles I'll get by.

He takes her hand and leads her to the window. They both look down into the busy street

See him?
Trish In the silver Merc?
Giles (*frowning*) Hava Jaffa — (*he shakes his head*) no, on the bench with the filthy mac and the bottle in a brown paper bag.
Trish I've seen him before.
Giles He lives in the street — topping up with milk and alcohol day and night.
Trish I feel sorry for them but what can you do?
Giles (*moving* C) Always been rather fascinated by meths drinkers, tramps, the dispossessed — that's the bottom line, Trish. That's what makes some of us well-fixed-up people wake up in a sweat of fear some nights. But I've always felt it might be a relief to fall that far — (*he laughs shortly*) to drop through all the layers laughing and cursing and discarding the trappings of one's wonderful "lifestyle" on the way.
Trish (*shocked*) I'm sure it's no relief when you hit the bottom — just horrible, frightening. (*She shudders*) I'd hate to be dirty like that, hair all sticky and ... urgh, I couldn't stand it.
Giles No, of course not — it's unthinkable.

They are both C, close. Trish stares at Giles

Trish Mr Short ——
Giles I've enjoyed the formality we've always maintained, Trish Evans, but you can call me Giles now if you wish.
Trish (*smiling*) Giles? (*She giggles*) I can't — it's like calling your teacher by his first name.
Giles (*shrugging*) What is it?
Trish I wonder, could we kiss?
Giles Kish, Trish? I mean, *kiss* Triss?
Trish (*giggling*) I know it's unusual but I've always wondered — like you said about doing me desperately over the copier. Lots of afternoons when you've been to lunch and it's been all drowsy and dusty and sunny in here I've stared across at you.
Giles Nodding at my desk, yes?
Trish (*nodding, giggling*) And I've wondered. Three years I've worked for you and we've never hardly touched; a peck on the cheek after the Christmas party; a rush of the fingers in passing the darts when we have a little game.

They are very close now but not touching

I'm a very tactile person, really — it's how I relate to people, you know?

Giles holds her by the elbows and she gasps softly

Giles This man who makes your heart leap when he comes into the room,
I hope he deserves you.
Trish Oh he does. (*Aching*) Can we kiss, Mr Short?
Giles Giles.
Trish I prefer Mr Short. Can we?
Giles Well, it doesn't look as if I'll be getting a present from the staff or a
golden handshake from the boss ...
Trish A golden kiss then.

*They kiss, almost chastely, delicately, with only their lips touching. They
break apart and she sighs. They stare at each other*

Can I ask you something?

Giles puts a finger on his lips and shakes his head then turns towards his desk

Giles Boxes, Trish?
Trish (*picking up the darts*) I hate that Font Cairns, always slagging people
off, writing his disgusting books! It's not fair.

*She throws darts into the cut-out as Giles looks on. All three stick in some part
of Cairns' anatomy*

I hate him!

*She goes to the door and opens it. Fergus shepherds Cairns into the office
like a precious walking antique. Trish goes out without a word*

Fergus Well now here we are, Font old chap, and here's Giles.

Fergus guides the stern and sullen Font across the room

I feel rather like an umpire at a duel. (*He chuckles falsely*) Soda syphons
at ten paces, gentlemen? Now let's see you two shake hands, eh?

Giles and Cairns regard each other warily

Cairns I'll press the flesh when he apologizes.
Fergus What do you say, Giles?

Pause. Then something seems to slacken in Giles' attitude and he sticks out a hand to Cairns

Giles Font, I apologize ——

Cairns takes his hand, triumph breaking on his face

—— for the drenching.

Fergus groans

Cairns And the scurrilous attack on my work? (*He snatches his hand away*) What about that!
Giles I meant every word, I'm afraid.
Cairns Damn you! You've been wasting my time, Fergus, I didn't come here to have my ego punctured twice in one day! (*He reels away and sees the darts sticking in the cut-out*) Look! I'm impaled! Well I think that says it all, don't you? *That's* what your beloved editor thinks of me.
Fergus (*glaring at Giles*) My ex-editor — he's fired!

Quivering with rage, they stand staring at Giles

Trish enters carrying a brown paper parcel, followed by Adrian, Melissa, three Office Workers and a beaming Monty, now with his campaign medals on, spruced up

Trish Time for the presentation, Mr Short.
Giles Trish, you shouldn't have — I'm not exactly going trailing clouds of glory.

The others gather in front of Giles

Trish It's for Monty.
Giles Ah, yes of course. (*Taking the parcel*) What is it?
Trish Tick-tock, tick-tock?
Giles A bomb — bit drastic, isn't it?
Trish (*hissing*) Clock!
Giles Well, Brownie points all round for originality. (*He coughs*)

Fergus and Cairns are detained by an air of expectancy as they all stare at Giles

Well, here we are then, Monty.

Monty (*saluting snappily*) All present and correct, Mr Short sah! Said we'd meet again, n'cetera, din' I, sah.

Giles Yes well, what can I say. I can only say: well done, bags of sterling snooping around and service to the firm. (*He shakes Monty's hand*) I'm happy to hand you this tribute from your friends and colleagues.

Trish (*leading the applause*) Well done, Monty!

Monty looks well miffed as the applause quickly peters out and his colleagues start a shuffle towards the door

Monty Snooping arahnd? Is that it? Twenny years I bin on that bladdy front door, opening it, shutting it, n'cetera, touching me cap n' saying goodmorning, n'cetera, good-evening, n'cetera, in all wevvers wiv me piles and me war wounds, n'cetera, and that's all you can say? *Is* that all you've got to say, Mister bleedin' Shortarse?

They all stop and stare

Giles Oh dear. (*Sadly*) Monty I ——

Monty Is that all you fink of me!

Giles No. I could say thank you for your unfailing surliness, the look of thinly veiled contempt you've always given me when I've arrived rather woozily back from lunch on occasions.

One of the Workers giggles

I could say thank God you're going and I won't be trapped in the lift or the corridor and have to endure your terminally boring monologue about being a POW, n'cetera. At times I've felt as if *I'd* spent half my life in a quarry near München Gladbach eating nothing but swedes and black bread — that's what I could say!

Trish (*soft aside*) You are saying it.

Giles (*through gritted teeth*) I know, God help me.

In the stunned aftermath Monty starts to wheeze and laugh

Monty Gord, you had me going for a minute there, Mr Short — I shoulda known you'd come up wiv' summink like this! You're a real joker intcha, squire?

The others laugh uneasily, relieved

Nar what you really got to say to old Monty, eh? Nar you got him by the testimonials so to speak?

Adrian groans and closes his eyes

Giles Monty Mason, you've been a boring old pain in the nether regions around here for far too long and I'm delighted you're leaving — even though my delight will be short-lived as it appears I'm leaving too.

The gathering applauds, mistakenly, half-laughing, half bewildered

    Good riddance, n'cetera!
Monty Do what? Do what? *Do what*!

Growling with fury Monty totters towards the open window and drops the parcel down into the street. There is a distinct cry and shouts and a car horn blowing from the street below. Trish, Melissa and Adrian rush to the window and look out. Cairns watches in horror. Fergus points at Giles from beside the door

Fergus Go, Giles! Leave the house of Rutherford as soon as you've cleared your desk!

Monty turns from the window and roars towards Giles like a small wounded grizzly throwing punches. Adrian tries to stop him and they both fall, knocking another Worker down as they go. They struggle on the floor. Giles stands c and laughs uncontrollably and Trish starts to cry beside him

 Black-out on the chaos

CURTAIN

ACT II

The same. About 3.30 p.m.

When the Curtain *rises, Giles is still musing* c, *but isolated. Gillette, a tramp, sits at Giles' desk with a bandaged head, looking dazed, and being tended by Trish. Fergus stands behind the tramp looking mortified. Adrian is pouring brandy into a tumbler. The parcel is now on Giles' desk, split open to reveal the smashed dome and works of a clock. Adrian approaches the threesome behind the desk and proffers a brimming glass of cognac*

Adrian Get that down you.

Fergus (*smoothly taking it and knocking it back in one*) Good man, Smethers.

Adrian (*stunned*) It was for him!

Fergus (*handing the tumbler back*) Ach. (*He glares at Giles*)

Adrian goes for a refill

(*Indicating Gillette*) If he sues us, Giles, it'll be on your head!

Gillette (*hopefully*) Whose head?

Fergus Sometimes I'm convinced the world is slowly returning to its original state. Primæval darkness, chaos, the swamp ——

Giles N'etcetera.

Gillette (*feeling his head tenderly*) Am I going to die?

Trish Of course not, you've had a nasty bump on the head that's all.

Gillette Damn. I thought I was a goner.

Trish You'll be as right as rain again soon Mr er ——?

Gillette Gillette.

Adrian (*with another brimming glass*) Ri-ight, you've had a bit of a close shave that's all — drink this.

Gillette I've had more close shaves than hot dinners. (*He starts to roll up a sleeve*) You wanna see my scars? I've got more scars than soft Mick ——

Trish (*pulling the sleeve back down*) No thank you.

Gillette (*taking the drink*) There I was, walking along wondering how to pass the time of day when it lands on me head — black-out. I fort: Thank God, I've 'ad an 'emmorage. It's all over at last.

Adrian I get the impression you're not a happy man, Mr Gillette.

Gillette Is it possible, sonny Jim? You show me an happy man and I'll show you someone who hasn't thought of the ramiferications of being alive.

Fergus Look here, Mr — er — Gillette, if you tell us where you live we can arrange for a taxi home — on the firm, of course.

Gillette (*a graveyard chuckle*) I can walk to my residence my little pink man: Park Hotel, Doorway B 'n' B — you needn't get me a taxi!

Fergus What's he talking about?

Trish I think he means he's homeless, Mr Rutherford, he sleeps in the street.

Giles He does, I've seen him.

Adrian (*moving away from Gillette*) God, he *hums*.

Giles goes up to Gillette

Giles *Mea culpa*, Mr Gillette. I'm to blame for your accident.

Gillette No hard feelings, squire, just wish you'd made a better job of it.

They all stare at him

Why did you bung the clock out the winder?

Giles *I* didn't.

Gillette You just said ——

Giles It was my fault, indirectly. I gave this (*indicating the clock*) to an employee and he threw it at you.

Gillette Must be nice to delegate your dirty work.

Giles I didn't tell him to throw it *at you* ——

Gillette Anybody passing'd do, eh? Having a bad day, were we, squire?

Giles sighs

Giles I'm sorry.

Gillette (*matter of fact*) Trouble is I'm a survivor. All I wanna do is cash in me chips but they keep refusing 'em. I've tried dozens of fings but do they work? (*He thinks*) I'm the man I couldn't kill.

Trish (*touched*) Mr Gillette, why on earth do you want to kill yourself?

Gillette (*dully amazed*) Isn't it bleedin' obvious? Look around you, gel.

Adrian I'd have thought Tower Bridge was a good bet.

Gillette Done it, son. Landed in a dredger full of sewage — you think I hum now?

Adrian It's pathetic anyway.

Gillette I jumped off the kitchen table once with the light flex tied round my neck — and the wires came out the walls. Whole place had to be rewired and plastered again — the bleedin' landlord kicked me out!

Adrian (*aside to Trish*) He's a nutcase.
Gillette Ran myself a bath full of water once.

He holds out the glass for more brandy. Adrian takes the glass

Plugged this electric fire into this socket on the landing and headed for the
bath with it. Be decent, I thought, they'll find me nice and clean in me pine
Radox — only the bleedin' thing wouldn't reach, would it.

Adrian sniggers and pours a drink

Story of my life that is, gentlemen — (*he smiles at Trish*) sweet lady. Too
short, wouldn't reach, not up to it, broke off at the crucial moment, bad
timing, bent in the middle. (*To Giles*) I've always fallen short, see guv?
Giles Yes, I know exactly what you mean.
Gillette Greeks have a saying: "Better Death than a bad fate" — I go along
with that.
Fergus Ach, what defeatist nonsense, man.
Gillette I write reg'lar to the Eufanasia Society for advice on how to get out
of it but all they keep saying is I don't qualify but keep in touch. I mean,
how bad do you have to be?
Adrian Have you tried stepping out in front of a bus?
Gillette Outside St Pancras. Closed me eyes when I seen it coming, stepped
out a bit late though and hit the side. Broke me ruddy snout, dazed meself
and this bleedin' kid helped me up on to a seat. I ended up at Mill Hill East,
for Gawd's sake! (*Incredulous still*) Mill Hill East. Took me two days to
get back to civilization.
Fergus (*heading for the door*) I can't listen to any more of this abysmal stuff
... (*He stops*) The world's full of opportunities if you've got the nous to see
them. Look *up*, man, get your mind out of the gutter and up to the windows
and rooftops! You must have had a job at some point. What were you?
Gillette Cat burglar, squire.

Fergus stares

Before that I was in insurance — General Accident.

Frances Feldman enters with a flourish, making them all look her way

Fran Giles, my poor darling. (*She crosses to embrace him*) I heard
something awful had happened to you so I flew here at once. What *has*
happened, my love?
Fergus My what? Giles, why is she addressing you like this?

Giles Well, er ——
Fran We're lovers, aren't we, Giles — of long and secret standing!
Giles Yes ...
Fergus My God, talk about flakes falling from one's eyes.
Fran (*noticing Gillette*) What's he doing here?
Gillette He clocked me one, Missis. (*He chuckles*) GBH from above with a timepiece.
Fran I thought you were some alcoholic writer. (*Back to Giles, intensely gushing*) Darling, I've had a tirade of abuse on the telephone from Verity so I know most of it. Is it true your marriage is over?
Giles It seems very likely unless ——
Fran Oh how marvellous, darling, so our time has come at last. Oh my all-darkness, my sweet — we're free!
Giles Freedom is terrible. I'd no idea ——
Fran I always knew this day would come, that fate would decree that you'd find the strength to leave that overgrown gymkhana pony of a wife of yours!
Giles Wife, house, job ——
Fran Job? Why?
Giles I offended the queen — the jewel in Rutherford's crown.
Fran It doesn't matter, my darling, you're a better writer than he'll ever be. I tell you there's nothing you won't be able to achieve with me by your side; you'll write *novels*, we'll travel the globe in search of inspiration, your talent will blossom; I'll introduce you to people — radical literary people, Giles! Our twin careers will zoom to the stars, my all-darkness ...

Giles looks rather embarrassed. Trish stares sadly at him. Fergus heads for the door again

Fergus I think they're putting something in the water. (*He stops*) The sooner you're out of this building the better, Giles. I fear for its very structure — I fear catastrophe.
Fran (*to Giles*) I have to go now, my wonderful, wonderful man, soulmate, my first and last love of my life, but I shall be back to pick you up.

Giles stares

You will be moving in with me, my angel?
Giles It's a strong possibility.
Fran What time will you be ready?
Giles Er ... (*Desperately looking at Trish*) I have to clear my desk and ——
Trish Just before six should be all right.
Giles Yes! Of course, all will be resolved by then — one way or the other.

Fran (*embracing him*) Until then, my love. Oh how wonderful to stand trembling on the brink of uncertainty, promise, hope — rebirth.
Gillette (*nudging Giles*) I broke into the swimming baths and stood trembling on the end of the top diving board once. I was sure I could see water down below but they'd covered the pool over for refurbishment and I ——
Fergus Smethers, will you arrange something for our guest? (*He gestures at Gillette behind his back:*) Get — him — out — of — here!
Fran Until just before six, my hero, my Che, my Tristan, my Tynan ——
Giles (*involuntarily*) N'cetera.
Fran Pardon?
Giles Nothing, it slipped out.
Fran Farewell!

With an ardent look at Giles, she goes

Fergus stands in the doorway and shakes his head at Giles sombrely

Fergus The world has gone mad with sex as my Highland forbears always said it would. I'd shake your hand, but one gets ever more wary of human contact.

Pause

Shafting the odd temp typist or barmy publisher's reader is one thing, but nobody shafts Fergus Rutherford. Goodbye, Giles. (*To Adrian*) Smethers.

Fergus goes. Adrian follows

Giles stands C, hit. Trish refills Gillette's glass

Trish Feeling a bit better?

Gillette knocks the drink back

Gillette (*regarding her*) You are a lovely creature, sweet lady.

Trish smiles. He looks at Giles' back

I hope you realize you got a gem here, squire? You got a pearl beyond price here.

Giles glances at Trish. Gillette starts to mumble and sing an indistinguishable monody to himself as the brandy takes effect. Throughout the following he continues singing gently and slurringly, between taking slugs of brandy

Trish You don't do things by halves, do you, Mr Short. Frances Feldman, your wife — I suppose you'll get a divorce. Seems such a shame. "The Shorts" — been like the kite mark as far as marriages go. You've been a rock, haven't you?

Giles Felt like a pile of rubble most of the time.

Trish All those years you've had with her, aren't they going to leave a terrible hole in your life? I mean, even with Miss Feldman and her all-darkness and stuff, are you sure you're doing the right thing?

Giles I'm no longer sure of anything. All my certainties have crumbled to dust.

Trish Tell me to mind my own business if you like but — *what was wrong*, Mr Short?

Giles (*thinking about it*) Ever heard of the ADPT?

Trish ADPT — not Roy Jenkins and Shirley Williams and that lot again is it?

Giles (*shaking his head*) The After Dinner Party Test — I invented it one night. Verity's a superb hostess and we'd had the latest of a string of successful dinner parties, but I was beginning to dread them because of afterwards.

Trish Afterwards!

Giles When the last laughing guests have gone and it's all been "Absolutely wonderful, darling", et cetera — (*he checks*) well, you close the door and turn to face the suddenly quiet house and ...

He is hit, turning sad and desolate before her eyes

Perhaps you fancy one more drink. She's by the dining-table surveying the ruination of the meal-taking, her back to you and tiredly unclipping her ear-rings. She turns, lovely, pleased at the way it's gone, glad that it's over and ready for the post-mortem on the guests' behaviour and ... (*He falters, full of pain*)

Trish And?

Giles Something awfully familiar resumes its grip on your life — a sad, hollow feeling; a sensation of ... falling short.

Trish Oh, Mr Short. (*Brimming with sympathy she almost reaches out but desists*) I am sorry.

Giles (*shrugging*) *Mea culpa*, I expect far too much.

Trish I think you do.

They both regard Gillette

Giles Something's broken his heart.

Trish Who was the temp typist Mr Rutherford mentioned?

Giles (*glancing at the copier*) I hope you don't think I make a habit of …
Trish Seducing your temps? No, you've been the perfect gent with me and
  I wondered ——

Adrian enters with Monty behind him looking truculent

Adrian Here we are then, Monty meet Mr Gillette.
Monty Him? I know him, he's always in the pubs rahnd here, scrounging
  and showing off his bleedin' scars, n'cetera. He stinks!

He takes Gillette roughly by the collar

  Let's have you aht of it, you old ferret!
Giles Take your hands off him ——

Monty glares at Giles, and looks to Adrian

Adrian Fergus said he had to go.
Trish (*going to Gillette's side*) I'll help Monty escort our guest to the door.

They get Gillette to his feet and head for door

Monty Then I'm going home — for good. (*He looks back at Giles*) See you
  down the Job Centre, *Mr* Short?
Gillette (*to Giles*) Been a pleasure to make your acquaintance, sir. I know
  a gentleman when I see one.
Giles Well, sorry again for the — er … (*He touches his head*)
Gillette Confluence of clock and crown? Ah don't think about it — time's
  always been a problem to me, squire. Time, heights, work, people,
  thinking, breathing, dogs, arithmetic — you might say the whole bleedin'
  package and have done with it.
Monty You're bleedin' idle that's your problem, bleedin' old dosser.
Gillette (*drawing himself up*) *I* had a profession, you jumped up little squit
  — and I was good at it until the vertigo got hold of me.

Monty barks contempt

Monty I read about you in the paper. You're the cat burglar what broke into
  the Kentucky Fried through a skylight and dropped straight into the vat,
  intcha?
Gillette I was dazzled by the lights.
Monty You was inebriated. A crowd gathered on the pavement outside and
  watched you climb out and go to the till — better than watching the tellies

in Currys they said! You were like a snail, they said, oozing across the floor!

Trish Come along, Mr Gillette.

Monty Fifty p in the till, wasn't there — *Raffles*?

Gillette (*with dignity*) One pound fifty, actually.

They head for the door. He looks back at Giles

You can't plan for to be happy, squire. It comes when you least expect it — surprises you it does.

Monty What would you know, you miserable git.

Gillette Not being happy is my subject. I got a degree from the Open University.

Giles I thought I was reasonably happy — until today.

Gillette Reasonably happy? What good's that? You might as well be reasonably alive.

Monty starts pushing him out

Monty Shaddap, you old tealeaf.

Monty shunts Gillette out of the door. Trish follows

Giles and Adrian regard each other. Giles walks to his desk with a cardboard box and opens a drawer

Giles I'd better start packing.

Adrian Giles, I want to ask you something.

Giles shakes his head, mimes cutting his throat

Why did you pick me out of the ruck? I didn't think I'd got a hope, all those Flash Harrys in their Armani suits. But you gave me the job.

Giles Planned any hols this year? I hear Goa's got a lot goan for it.

Adrian Why me, Giles?

Giles (*sadly*) Melissa asked me.

Adrian stares, hit

She loved you, she wanted you to succeed. Anyway, I felt you'd do a good job and you have — I made the right choice.

Adrian My wife canvassed you. (*He thinks*) Knowing Melissa she *lobbied* you remorselessly.

Giles Doesn't matter.

Adrian (*pacing before Giles, musing*) More of a hounding, I bet. She is a determined person: if she wants something she makes her case known.

Giles Please, forget it.

Adrian She's already on to me about putting in for fiction editor.

Giles A wife should have her husband's interests at heart.

Adrian stops pacing and stares at Giles

Adrian She was only your temp.

Giles How about a last game of darts?

Adrian She still goes into a kind of reverie about those days when she was a temp under the great Giles Short.

Giles God, the England cricket selectors want a shake-up, don't they? They want boiling in beeswax — or linseed oil.

Adrian (*worrying away at it*) She was under pressure at the time, I wasn't working and we were trying like hell for a kid — upside down, hanging from the chandeliers to try and get a bull's-eye. We were so desperate.

Giles You must be thrilled it worked then; I'm so happy for you both.

Adrian Giles, I have to ask you something of the utmost ——

Giles goes into a fake coughing fit, bad and prolonged enough for Adrian to pat him on the back

(*Finally*) Did you and ——

Verity enters looking determined

Verity Giles ... (*She stops*) Oh hallo Adrian, how's Melissa?

Adrian (*dully*) She's ... Fine, I think.

Verity You think? You must look after *them* now, you know. I always think it's unfair that the woman has all the carrying to do — there should be some way of sharing it.

Giles (*mildly*) They should become United Carriers you mean? Like the haulage firm.

Adrian What would either of you know about it? (*Heading for door; darkly*) You've no children of your own — as far as we know!

He goes out slamming the door

Verity What is the matter with him?

Giles Oh, er — he found out Melissa asked me to look favourably on his job prospects. Years ago, irrelevant of course.

Verity And you did?

Pause. He nods

But you're usually so scrupulous about things like that. (*She strolls to the window*)

Giles I felt sorry for them.

Verity Jaffa's outside in a Mercedes with an orange logo on the side — what a vulgar sight.

Giles I don't see why he has to keep tabs on me.

Verity (*moving closer, staring at him*) Was Melissa good at it?

Giles *It?*

Verity Temping?

Giles No, to be honest — and we both know I must. Her typing was — Wagnerian — and talk? I've heard of verbal diarrhoea but she has dysentery.

Verity (*thinking*) Lovely girl though.

Giles (*airily*) I suppose so. How are things at home?

Verity Oddly calm except Morag's got flu and is lying in her garret like a snuffling lump of misery trying to make me look after her. Well sod it, she's the au pair not me!

Pause. She wanders to the copier. Giles watches. She strokes a finger along the top of the machine

Melissa … You must have got to know her pretty well …

Giles shrugs

Did you "get to know her"?

Giles Oh God, Verity …

Verity Were you "temp'ted", Giles? Did something start to stir beneath your nice old pedestal desk one somnolent afternoon?

He stares in horror

Trish comes into the doorway carrying a file

Verity does not see her

Or was it lunchtime the blinds went down and the door was locked and you cleared the end of your desk for a desk-ender. (*Her voice rising*) Or did you just pull her knickers off and have her on the office carpet, Giles? Did you shag her? (*Shouting in fury*) Did you?

Trish Sorry, Mr Short. (*She starts to back out again*)
Verity Oh don't withdraw, girl! We're not talking about you — at least I hope
     not — I don't think my mind could cope with the thought of him screwing
     someone called Trish at any remove.

Trish looks hit

     No come in, come in — Shagger Short here is going to give us a list of his
     conquests, aren't you, darling?
Giles There's no need to drag Trish into this.
Verity So! There's someone besides the office cat you haven't shagged!
     Well done! But what about Melissa? Come on, you've got to tell the truth
     — has she been given a short, sharp shag, *darling*!

*Pause. The two women stare at Giles. He takes a breath and opens his mouth
to answer*

Black-out

SCENE 2

The same. Two hours later

*The Lights come up on Giles and Verity sitting at opposite sides of his desk
which is cleared of all but their cups of coffee. Trish has gone and her
computer is covered up, etc. Obviously things have calmed down. A long
moment*

Verity (*finally*) How little we've really known each other. A decade of
     marriage and all this (*glancing at the copier*) has been going on. It *does
     hurt*, Giles.
Giles I'm desperately sorry.
Verity What is it about that machine? (*She stares at the copier again*)
     Symbol of reproduction or something? (*Pause*) Don't tell me it was "just
     an arrangement", that you "did it as a favour" — don't insult my
     intelligence.
Giles It wasn't my idea. And Adrian has no idea.
Verity I bet you didn't take much persuading!
Giles (*gently*) No.

*Verity gets up and paces the room, pondering. She finds herself close to the
copier, stares at it in distaste then goes to the window*

Giles If I haven't told you about Fran and this *tiny* fling with Melissa ——

She turns and glares at him

> — and I haven't of course — it's partly because I detest those men who have affairs then tell their wives in order to ease their conscience.

Verity How noble of you! (*Pause*) What's the rest of the reason?

Giles (*shrugging*) Shit scared I guess.

Verity I'd no idea your desire to reproduce was so strong.

Giles It isn't.

Verity I could have had children — I have childbearing hips, all the equipment — I'd have had litters if I'd known you wanted to so bad. I still might.

Giles I wanted them to have a child not me.

Verity Oh! In her job description was it? In your diary: "Tuesday p.m., impregnate temp sec." Just who the hell do you think you are!

She glares at Giles who looks anguished

> You'll go down and down without me. I'll pass this grizzled old man on a park bench and realize it was you.

Giles That kind of existence isn't as far away as we like to think.

Verity Nonsense! We deserve our comfortable existence — we've worked and slaved for it

Giles (*mildly*) I've worked, darling, you've shopped.

Verity I've kept the house, been the Hostess with the Mostest — I've done what we agreed!

He takes her hand for a moment

> I'm not having a very nice time, you know! There are men outside the house in a van — swarthy men reading the *Sun* and eating things in pitta bread! And I've been so miserable, wandering about picking things up and putting them down again — our lovely things, Giles: the furniture, the flower arrangements in lovely vases. I love our things, you know that ...

Giles But they are just *things*, Verity.

Verity I haven't phoned Mummy and Daddy yet but I shall have to. Daddy will know what to do.

Giles nods wearily

> I'm afraid they'll say they were right about you, darling.

Giles Why break the habit of a lifetime?

Verity What do you mean?

Giles They've never stopped telling you what a mistake you made marrying me.

Verity Well! Melissa Lacy Drawers! Frances "Knicker Elastic" Feldman whom I'd have trusted with my life! Daddy said you were nothing but a rake after that first weekend when he caught you in my bedroom — and he was bang on!

Giles I've been a disappointment, I agree.

Verity You damn well have!

Giles (*shrugging*) What could I do to impress parents who obviously wanted a cross between Michael Portillo and a gundog for their son-in-law?

Verity They knew what you were!

Pause

What's it all been *for*, Giles? Why did we stay together as most of our friends fell apart? We've both got our moods but we always came round eventually.

Giles After a few days in hell.

Verity Yes! But we did, we've been sensible ——

He sighs

— too sensible, is that it? Is that why you went to Fran? Is she sexy? I just can't see it but I suppose she must be. I need to know where I went wrong.

Giles You did not go wrong.

Verity Tell me the truth! What was missing that you had to go crawling to that Bohemian rhapsody of a false friend of mine!

Giles remains mute, pained, shaking his head

God, you're like that bloody toy dalmatian Mummy has in the Range Rover! Stop it and answer my question!

Giles I think ... Perhaps we expect too much of everything, we're not reasonable in our expectations of life: it has to be wonderful — especially relationships, especially love — that's the top prize, isn't it? That's the really quite rare conjunction of true minds we expect to be as available as washing powder.

Verity What's been wrong with us! *I* haven't been screwing around! Come on, Giles I don't want bits out of books.

Giles Surely you've felt something missing? A lack of something?

Verity (*after a thoughtful pause*) There have been times. Been out, y' know ... Tea and buns and shopping with some of the gels — chatter chatter, everything's wonderful, darling, et cetera.

Giles blinks

Then you bustle back into the house and put your parcels down and …
(*Pause. A heaviness fills her*) It evaporates somehow, you look at the
Hermes scarf and the new suit and can't even be boshed to put them in the
wardrobe. The day just seems too long and you want to lie on the bed and
suck your thumb and cry. (*She starts to snuffle a bit*)

Giles goes to her, holds her at arms' length. They kneel

Giles That *is* the feeling. It's wonderful to hear you admit we haven't been
living in a TV advert. Verity, I think this awful bet might free us both —
give us back our sense of reality?
Verity I hope you're not going to suggest we might be happy in a semi —
in Pinner with a Ford Fiesta outside?
Giles A semi in Pinner? I was thinking I'd drink meths and you'd be my
baglady — Harrods' bags, of course.

She laughs. They both laugh a little

Verity It hasn't been all bad, has it? We've always shared a sense of humour,
haven't we?
Giles Oh *yes*, we've had great times.
Verity "Had". Is it all past tense now? Is it over for you, Giles?
Giles You said don't come back ——
Verity Oh, I'd have you back, you bugger! The other thing's just too painful.
Rattling round that damn great house on my own I …

She notices his smile

It would have to be on different terms, of course.

Giles stares. They are close together on the carpet

You'd have to be a reformed character: settle down, no more gambling or
fornicating — except with me, of course.
Giles We'd play cards together?
Verity I'm serious! I'd want all of you — every damn bit, no shortchanging
me in any way!
Giles We might have nowhere to live.
Verity We could live with Mummy and Daddy for a while ——
Giles Oh God!

Suddenly Verity is hugging and trying to kiss him in front of the copier

Verity I'll do it, Giles, I'll do anything you want — I'm not a prude, you'll see. You can take me now if you like, darling.

She is pulling him on top of herself. Giles has his jacket pushed back to his elbows and is shaking his head

Frances enters with her usual brio wearing a big rakish hat

Fran What's this Giles? One for the road?
Verity Oh shit.

They get up

Giles Fran ... (*Struggling to put his jacket on*) Er ... An offer I was trying to refuse, actually.
Fran Are you ready? I've got the car outside but it's on a meter.
Verity (*to Giles*) You're going to her? You had it arranged. (*She laughs bitterly*) I've been such a fool: coming here, thinking I had something to ... (*Shouting in his face*) Go then, Shagger Short, and I hope I never see you again!
Giles I'm not going anywhere yet. (*He checks the clock*) One of the conditions is that I do my usual routine.
Verity (*heading for the door, glaring at Frances*) I hope you'll be deeply unhappy together!
Fran "All's fair in love and war", Verity.

Verity stops beside Frances

Verity You rutting cow ——
Fran Oh come now, let's be civilized about this ——
Verity Civilized! Don't spout clichés at me. You're a walking cliché as it is!
Fran *I'm* a cliché? Have you looked in a shop window lately, Mrs Perfect Hostess Sloaney Frump of the Year?
Verity (*stunned*) You — Judas bitch. You were my best friend, my confidante. Don't think I don't know why you lured him (*she glances at Giles*) away!
Fran It was love the moment I saw him on my step with a manuscript under one arm and snowflakes on his hair.

Verity puts two fingers in her mouth and makes retching noises

Verity (*to Giles*) How can you put up with this stuff?
Fran (*going to Giles and hanging on his shoulder*) Oh he puts up with it very

well, don't you, darling heart? (*Nuzzling his ear*) Puts up with it at every opportunity, in fact — if you'll forgive the grammar.

Verity (*approaching them*) Oh, I bet he does. I do remember, y' know? (*To Frances, close now*) I trusted you, you long past, sell-by date *vamp*. I felt disloyal afterwards but I told you, didn't I? And you were so kind, so bloody coo-ingly supportive. I'll never forgive you!

Giles (*puzzled*) For what?

Fran Nothing, darling. (*To Verity*) How your bourgeois scruples amused me! Hah!

Verity Nothing to a woman of your experience obviously!

Giles What is this about?

Fran She told me things ——

Verity I should have kept to myself.

Fran I could hardly keep a straight face! They weren't terribly unusual, darling, I swear.

Verity We'd only been married three years!

Fran Hah! I'd done them when I was a teenager but then I've always had imagination.

Verity In the dark behind the disco, I suppose?

Fran Oh never! I love the lights on! (*She laughs. Imitating Verity*) "There are things Giles wants to do in bed I just can't *countenance*, Fran — I'd never be able to make my Confession again!"

Verity Now I know why you just looked rather thoughtful for a while! You randy, bluestocking bitch ——

Fran You *Country Life*, horsey frump! I can't understand what he ever saw in you!

Verity Only too obvious what he saw in you, you arty-farty, Kama Sutra shagbag!

Giles (*shocked*) For heaven's sake ——

Verity (*turning on him*) So many things have slipped into place today, Giles! How could you betray me with — that? What does it feel like to leave *that* in the early hours and slip between the sheets with me murmuring: "Oh I'm so cold, Verity, warm me"?

Giles Desolate. Guilt-ridden. Driven and longing for forgiveness — to be taken back into the fold.

Fran (*to him*) You've never told me this.

Giles It's too pathetic. When I'm with you I want her a little bit; when I'm with her I want you a little bit and when I'm on my own I want you both. I've been splitting in two for years! (*He stares from one to the other*) I'm not making excuses, but it's been hell.

Fran grabs Giles by the arm and pulls him towards the door

Fran You're coming to my flat, darling — I'll make you whole again, succour you.

Verity (*taking his other arm and holding them back*) Giles! That man can't possibly take the house or anything else, I'm sure — a verbal wager won't stand up in a court of law! I will make our marriage work, darling. I want you — you're mine!

They see-saw back and forth with Giles in the middle

Fran } (*shouting together*) { Let go of my lover!
Verity } { Get off my husband! (*Etc.*)

Fergus enters angrily with a subdued Trish close behind

They stop

Fergus Ladies! What is going on here? You're disrupting the entire firm!

Three curious Workers' faces peer around the door frame

Trish goes to her desk and picks up her jacket and bag without a word

You still here, Giles?

Giles (*seeing Trish*) Yes. Trish, I thought you'd gone home.

Trish (*going to the door with her jacket and bag*) I'm going now, Mr Short. Goodbye.

Fergus Good-night, lassie.

Trish goes out. The Workers' faces withdraw

She's been with me for hours pleading your case, but it's no use — I want you off these premises.

Fran } (*together*) He's coming with me.
Verity }

Verity Fergus, please? Reconsider?

Fergus shakes his head

The door opens and Hava Jaffa appears, smiling, enigmatic, juggling an orange in one hand

Jaffa So, went the day well?

Giles Well? I haven't lied but I've lost my job, my good reputation, several friends and — (*he stares at the two women*) I haven't a clue what to do next.
Jaffa You have proved yourself an honourable man — to me at least.

The clock now shows 5.50 p.m.

(*He checks his chunky gold watch*) In ten minutes all will be as it was.
Giles Hah! Things will never be the same — I've blown my life to bits.
Verity (*to Jaffa*) How could you do this to my husband? Haven't you got a heart?
Jaffa You know, since I came to England as a young man I have looked for a man of honour, a true English gentleman.
Giles I'm not that by any stretch of the imagination. If I could go back I think I'd lie through my teeth — religiously. Truth destroys!
Jaffa Hasn't it been interesting? (*Smiling and deftly juggling the orange, he strolls around the room. He stops in front of Fergus*) Cairns will come back.

Fergus stares

Despite everything he wants to be thought of as a good writer, he longs for respect. Besides, I have obtained some rather interesting postcards of him — from Morocco. (*He goes on and stops in front of Frances*) You must be ... Giles? Introduce?
Giles Frances Feldman, a friend ——

Jaffa lifts an eyebrow

— and mistress of many years standing ——
Verity And lying and sitting and in the backs of taxis and swinging from lamp-posts, I shouldn't wonder!
Fran I'm a redblooded woman not a missionary-position, milk-and-water frump!
Giles Stop it! (*He stares at Jaffa*) How did you know about Cairns?

Jaffa smiles and feels behind Giles' lapels to produce two tiny listening devices

Jaffa There are no flies on you, Giles, but a couple of bugs maybe. (*He slips them into a pocket*) I always hedge my bets. I hear everything (*glancing at the window*) from outside.
Giles There was no need for that — trust you said.
Fergus What can you expect from an unprincipled, foreign rogue! Now will you all leave!

Jaffa Rutherford, you are a short-sighted fool ——

Fergus Optically challenged if you don't mind! (*Pointing commandingly at the bathroom door*) There's the door!

Jaffa To the bathroom. (*He claps Giles on the back, chuckling*) Cheer up, my friend, you have almost won, and shown yourself to be a man of truly liberal conscience — a kind, good man.

Giles (*shaking his head*) I don't know what to do.

Verity Come home, Giles, since it appears we still have one. (*To Jaffa*) Hard luck, you vampire!

Fran You can't go back to that — domesticity, Giles! Break out! Come with me, my all-darkness.

Fergus Oh hell's flames!

They all stare at him

I really don't want to start looking for another bloody fiction editor.

Verity hugs and kisses Fergus

Verity Oh bless you, Fergus! Oh Giles, isn't that wonderful, darling.

Fergus There'll have to be a new contract — with a clause forbidding the telling of truth.

The clock shows 5.55 p.m.

Adrian enters pulling a reluctant Melissa by the hand

Adrian I want the truth!

Giles (*groaning*) Haven't we had enough for one day ...

Adrian stops c and pushes Melissa towards Giles

Adrian There he is! The sperm bank of Covent Garden!

Giles Adrian ——

Adrian Don't Adrian me! I admired you, I respected you, liked you immensely — loved you almost, I'm not ashamed to say it — but I loathe you now, you — office carpet shagger! How could you?

All eyes focus on Giles. He stares at Melissa

Melissa Giles, tell him it's not true. He's gone mad, smashed up the nursery and dragged me here — please tell him!

Giles Tell him what?

Melissa That nothing happened between us when I was your temp. (*She holds her belly with both hands*) Tell him that this isn't anything to do with you?

Adrian It all fits! The dates are right: the last time your secretary took her hols and she (*jabbing a finger at Melissa*) came back to cover. That's when it was done, Mr High and Mighty Short, wasn't it?

Adrian starts to break up and Melissa goes to hold him. She looks at Giles with eyes full of pleading

Giles Nothing happened.

Adrian slowly looks up

(*With absolute conviction*) I didn't touch your wife, Adrian — the child is yours and hers.

Adrian Do you *swear*?

Giles On my honour.

Adrian stares, wanting desperately to believe

Adrian Giles?

Giles I refer my honourable friend to the reply I gave a moment ago. (*Nobly*) I'm hurt that you could think it of me.

Adrian Dark thoughts. I'm sorry, Giles.

Melissa Thank you, Giles.

Adrian (*sticking out a hand*) No hard feelings.

Giles None. (*He grins*)

Melissa and Adrian go out quickly and Fergus follows

Six o'clock chimes and everyone looks towards the clock

It's over.

Giles looks at Hava Jaffa who is C

It's all yours, I'll make the arrangements.

Fran What? (*She glances at the door*) You mean you lied? How could you?

Giles With ease, sincerity — and an enormous sense of relief. I'm back in the real world, thank God.

He sees Jaffa taking his mobile phone out of his pocket and dialling

What are you doing?

Jaffa (*moving to the window*) I have some men standing by.

Verity I knew it! Have they got sledgehammers to break down the doors? I hate you, Hava Jaffa. I hate your stupid name!

Jaffa (*moving back to* C) You know, when the Allies reached our sub-section of Matthausen there were only about a hundred or so of us left: children, and the old — the leftovers, too far gone to walk out of the gates, propped against walls and each other like stooks of corn, waiting to die. A soldier, with tears running down his honest English face, started handing out oranges from a sack. Oranges. Dropping into skeletal palms (*cupping his palms*) like suns, smelling of health, sanity, deliverance. At last he came to me. He looked so robust I was afraid of him; he shone with health above me. "What's your name, son?" he asked and I realized I didn't know, didn't have one. Been through so much, seen so much, the tape was wiped clean. I was a stare, a nothing, a no-name. "Have a Jaffa," he said and dropped the world into my hands again, gave me my life again, my futurity. (*He drops the orange into Verity's hands*) "Have a Jaffa." Hence, my name. (*He dials a number. Into the mobile phone*) Hava Jaffa here. Leave it, go home. ... No, the job is over — thank you.

Giles Does this mean ... The bet ——

Jaffa — is closed, Giles. Despite what people seem to think, I am not a greedy — foreigner. (*He heads for door, reaches it, and turns. His dark-eyed gaze sweeps across their faces. With childlike simplicity*) All the riches of the world are not worth a single moment of life — and could not buy one.

Jaffa exits, leaving the door open

Verity Let's go home, darling ——

Fran Giles, come with me ——

Giles stares at them, torn

Trish enters shyly

Giles stares at her as if seeing her for the first time. She stops just inside the doorway

Trish Mr Short ...

Giles Yes, Trish?

Trish I'm sure it's ridiculous, if not barmy, but it came to me on the Tube and I couldn't get rid of it. Goodge Street I'd got to, and thinking what I'd give Gran for her tea and all that, but I kept thinking: it's been a funny old day, turned inside out sort of day. Truth and honesty and ...

Verity Out with it, girl! What are you wittering about?

Trish (*caving in, about to flee*) I just thought for once I'd ask for something — for myself.

Giles Ask then.

Trish I'd just like you to know — Giles — that if you're stuck, Gran and me used to take in lodgers when she was able.

Verity Oh how sweet! Lodgers!

She and Fran snigger with amusement. Then they notice Giles is staring past them at Trish who backs to the doorway, embarrassed, belittled

Giles Are you sure about this, Trish?

Trish Oh yes, there's plenty of room.

Giles walks across the room to Trish. Verity and Fran gape

Verity Giles, what are you doing? This is absurd.

Fran This is grotesque, Giles: not your little *secretary*?

Giles takes Trish by the hand and looks back at his wife and mistress

Verity ⎱
            ⎰ (*together*) Giles, *why?*
Fran

Giles looks down into Trish's upturned, shining face then at the staring, indignant, shocked ones

Giles (*simply*) The heart leaps.

He and Trish exit into the late golden sunlight like adult Start-rite kids

Fran and Verity are stunned for a moment, then lift their hands to their faces and start to wail like women at a Greek funeral

Black-out

CURTAIN

FURNITURE AND PROPERTY LIST

ACT I
SCENE 1

On stage: **Giles'** desk. *On it*: phone, file tray, papers, manuscripts, etc. *In drawer*: set of darts, various other items
Trish's desk. *On it*: word processor, papers, files, folder containing readers' reports with mauve envelope attached to one
2 desk chairs
2 chairs
Photocopier (practical). *Beside it*: packet of paper
Life-sized cut-out of Font Cairns. *Around it*: piles of *Brains on Toast*
Shelves. *On them*: books
Butler's tray. *On it*: glasses, various bottles of drink, soda syphon
Coat stand
Large wall clock (set at 6 a.m. to start)
Dartboard on wall
Book posters on walls
Venetian blinds (closed) at window
Carpet

Off stage: Practical torch (**Monty**)
Plastic cup of coffee (**Monty**)

Personal: **Jaffa**: chunky gold watch, orange in pocket
Giles: wrist-watch

SCENE 2

Re-set: Wall clock at 9 a.m.
Venetian blinds open fully

Set: **Giles'** jacket on back of chair

Off stage: Handbag (**Trish**)
Glass of orange juice, Anadin (**Trish**)

Personal: **Giles**: Ray-Ban sunglasses in pocket
Adrian: red spectacles (worn throughout)

A L<small>IGHTING</small> DIMS ON PAGE 10

Re-set: Wall clock at 10 a.m.

Off stage: Briefcase, copy of *The Times* (**Fergus**)
              2 expensive shopping bags, handbag (**Verity**)

S<small>CENE</small> 3

Re-set: Wall clock at 11.30 a.m.

Set: Bucket of ice on drinks tray

Personal: **Cairns**: glass of gin and tonic
              Trish: handkerchief

S<small>CENE</small> 4

Re-set: Wall clock at 3 p.m.

Off stage: Clock wrapped in brown paper parcel (**Trish**)

Personal: **Monty**: military medals

ACT II
S<small>CENE</small> 1

Re-set: Wall clock at 3.30 p.m.

Set: Split parcel with smashed clock on **Giles'** desk
              Cardboard box

Off stage: File (**Trish**)

S<small>CENE</small> 2

Strike: All items from **Giles'** desk top

Re-set: Wall clock at 5.30 p.m.
              Trish's handbag and jacket on her desk
              Cover on computer

Set: 2 cups of coffee on **Giles**'s desk

Personal: **Jaffa**: mobile phone
                 Giles: 2 tiny bugging devices behind lapels

LIGHTING PLOT

Property fittings required: nil
Interior. The same scene throughout

ACT I, SCENE 1. 6 a.m.

To open: Very dim lighting, early morning light from window

Cue 1	**Jaffa** partly opens the blinds	(Page 1)
	Increase lighting, gradually increasing as scene progresses	
Cue 2	**Giles**: "What have I done?"	(Page 5)
	Black-out	

ACT I, SCENE 2. 9 a.m.

To open: General interior lighting, with daylight from window

Cue 3	**Trish** starts to operate the copier	(Page 10)
	Dim lighting; when ready bring up full general lighting	
Cue 4	**Giles** takes aim again	(Page 19)
	Black-out	

ACT I, SCENE 3. 11.30 a.m.

To open: General interior lighting, with daylight from window

Cue 5	**Trish** dashes out after them, giggling	(Page 26)
	Black-out	

ACT I, SCENE 4. 3 p.m.

To open: General interior lighting, with daylight from window

Cue 6	**Giles** laughs uncontrollably and **Trish** cries	(Page 36)
	Black-out	

ACT II, SCENE 1. 3.30 p.m.

To open: General interior lighting, with afternoon sunlight from window

Cue 7   **Giles** opens his mouth to answer   (Page 47)
               Black-out

ACT II, SCENE 2. 5.30 p.m.

To open: General interior lighting, with late afternoon sunlight from window

Cue 8   **Fran** and **Verity** start to wail   (Page 58)
               Black-out

EFFECTS PLOT

ACT I

Cue 1   To open   (Page 1)
City street noise from below, intermittent at first, gradually increasing

Cue 2   Black-out   (Page 5)
Cut street noise; when ready bring up bustling street sound to open Scene 2; *continue throughout*

Cue 3   **Trish** turns to the computer   (Page 9)
Phone

Cue 4   **Giles** opens the window   (Page 19)
Increase street noise

Cue 5   Black-out   (Page 19)
Cut street noise; when ready bring up bustling street sound to open Scene 3; *continue throughout*

Cue 6   Black-out   (Page 26)
Cut street noise; when ready bring up bustling street sound to open Scene 4; *continue throughout*

Cue 7   **Fergus** puts the receiver down   (Page 26)
Phone

Cue 8   **Fergus** drums his fingers on the desk   (Page 26)
Phone

Cue 9   **Monty** drops the parcel down into the street   (Page 36)
Cry, shouts, car horn blowing from street below

ACT II

Cue 10   To open Scene 1   (Page 37)
City street noise from below

Cue 11   Black-out   (Page 47)
Cut street noise; when ready bring up bustling street sound to open Scene 2; *continue throughout*

Cue 12   **Melissa**, **Adrian** and **Fergus** go out   (Page 56)
Clock chimes six